THINK
BEFORE
YOU WINK

A Practical Guide for the Successful Christian Single

Andy & Helen Yawson

Published by

Illumination House

P.O. Box DS1277 - Dansoman - Accra - Ghana

Email: illumination_house@yahoo.com

ISBN 978-9988-1-6787-5

TABLE OF CONTENTS

FOREWORD

The subject of relationships that lead to marriage could be likened to the knotting of a tie. The quality of a tie is almost often traced to the quality of the knot. It will determine if it's a short or long tie. It will be the reason for the tie being crooked or straight, acceptable or not.

In this book Andy and Helen have left almost no stone unturned in trying to help people going into relationship, to do it right from the beginning. In certain parts of the world where young people are practically set up by parents or spiritual leaders to choose certain persons, they help us to see the power of the friendship factor.

They have done a good work in showing us that an imbalanced relationship can end up hurting us in the future. Imbalance is a pointer to an abomination. However, when the two people are committed to laying a good foundation, the future of bliss is guaranteed.

The richness of the content of the book would make it a good guide for intending couples and a practical book on the syllabus of couples' fellowships.

Pastor Matthew Ashimolowo
President/Senior Pastor
Kingsway International Christian Centre (KICC)

PREFACE

Think Before You Wink takes a biblical and practical down-to-earth approach on the issues of how to handle relationships as a Christian Single.

Most Pastors' and Counsellors' offices are full of people who are dealing with the consequences of the good, not-so good and downright ridiculous decisions they may have made regarding their relationships.

This book offers guidance to the Christian single whilst challenging a number of popular and long-standing myths that have crept into the life of the modern day Christian.

The life of the Christian Single is meant to be fun and enjoyable and this book ensures that we have that fun whilst making good quality decisions that will define our future.

Andy and Helen Yawson

INTRODUCTION

The subject of relationships, especially between the opposite sexes, in our society has always been a hotly debated issue because it invokes various reactions from different facets of our society.

As Christians, however, we have to deal with another level of complexity when it comes to relationships as we seek to obey and honour God in everything we do whilst being bombarded with various ideas, some of which may even be contrary to God's word. The practicing Christian is desirous that his or her entire life honours God so we come to the subject of relationships from this premise:

> *Colossians 3:23-24 (NKJV) - "And whatever you do, do it heartily, as to the Lord and not to men, knowing that from the Lord you will receive the reward of the inheritance; for you serve the Lord Christ."*

Christians are to recognize that our obedience to God should take precedence over the culture and values of the earthly society we live in.

Today's Christian is however dealing with another challenge which has been created by the church community itself – mainly unconsciously and if not handled well can result in challenges in our future relationships and certainly marriage.

Many young Christian men and women will attest to the fact that once you are seen walking or talking jovially with a member of the opposite sex, you get the reaction from church people that your dealings with this person:

[1] ought to lead to a marriage proposal very soon or

[2] is sinful or about to be sinful!

I must also add that most pastors will readily agree that majority of the issues that end up in their counselling rooms have a lot to do with relationships between the opposite sexes. It seems that ever since Adam and Eve had issues with God over how they managed their relationship, we are still trying to find workable solutions that will ensure that we have fruitful relationships with God as well as with the opposite sex!

This book offers some guidance to the 21st century Christian single as he or she navigates through the maze we call relationships with the opposite sex.

A relevant study guide at the end of each chapter will ensure that it can be used for personal study or effective material for group study and discussions. It is our prayer that you will find the contents revealing, refreshing and relevant.

#1
CAN'T WE JUST BE FRIENDS?

The tendency for church people to speculate that any interaction between Christian singles is meant to lead to romantic relationship has left most frustrated singles asking whether there is anything wrong with having a friend of the opposite sex. Others have been so affected by this that they tend not to develop any form of friendship with those of the opposite sex as they grow up.

As a result of this, most young men and women who may not have developed healthy friendships with the opposite sex, but would want to end all the speculation and the subtle pressure that the church puts on them, tend to marry the first person they befriend.

The problem here though is this: if you have not learnt how to relate with a member of the opposite sex in a healthy manner with no strings attached, how well are you going to do if you enter courtship with the first person you befriend?

There have been many cases of young men and women making the choice of their marriage partner the focus of their life, once they get into a tertiary institution because of the popular myth that if they don't succeed in doing so whilst on the university campus, their chances will be gloomier after they graduate. This has even affected some people's studies and in other cases, people have made commitments to others about marriage whilst on campus, only to graduate and realize that it was done in haste. In the worst case, they marry and then get fed up very quickly, consigning both of them to a life of strife and frustration.

The other major cause of this challenge is that most young men and women, when they become born-again Christians, are taught that in order for them to live holy lives as singles it is advisable to avoid relating to the opposite sex. Some have even gone to the extreme of telling young men to be wary of the ladies in church else 'the devil might use the ladies to cause their downfall'! This has contributed to a lot of Christian men having little or no experience of any healthy friendships with the opposite sex by the time they get to the stage of considering who to marry.

As you read this, I want you to know that there are a lot of benefits to be derived from having healthy friendships with the opposite sex before settling on the issue of marriage, and I hope to mention a few.

I also want to emphasize on the adjective 'healthy' because it is only in healthy friendships that one can fully benefit.

10 SIGNS OF A HEALTHY FRIENDSHIP

1. People are friends because they both want to be. No one is feeling compelled to be in the friendship. We see a good example in the Bible of the kind of friendship that developed between David and Jonathan – no one felt compelled to befriend the other.

2. There is no domination or manipulation by one party in the friendship. When one party starts to behave as if you are obliged to maintain the friendship at all cost, it becomes unhealthy.

   It should not be a case where if I don't attend Mary's party, it is going to be World War III; although I really cannot make it, but I have to do it to save our friendship. Worse still, Mary has decided that we should all wear pink to the function, whether male or female and I have to follow suit or else that will be the end of the friendship. That is manipulation.

3. Friends are free to be unpredictable in the friendship. They can be themselves.

4. Friends in a healthy friendship are free to express their opinion – they are free to voice out their disagreements at any time. For example, a number of men who have never had female colleagues disagreeing with them on any issue before, find it difficult to handle it when they get into courtship or marriage, and resort to all sorts of 'interesting' interpretation of scripture, to try and wrongfully subdue their wives when they object to something. This is unhealthy!

5. Each person in this friendship is free to have personal plans for their lives. They don't feel compelled to have their plans approved by the other party before they go ahead.

6. Friends are not possessive. They do not act as if they own each other. If the other person is just a friend, then you have no right questioning them every time you see them talking to other people. This attitude, even in courtship, is unhealthy and has destroyed many friendships and courtships.

7. Each friend keeps a separate identity within the friendship

8. They encourage each other to become all that they are capable of becoming.

9. People have both individual and shared goals.

10. People do not intentionally 'use' each other. In this kind of friendship, friends are not scheming on what they can squeeze out of each other. Although one friend may be more well off than the other, the less advantaged doesn't feel intimidated by the other and is not overly dependent on his or her friend.

Having listed some of the signs of a healthy friendship let us now look at some guidelines on biblical ways to develop these healthy friendships, especially with the opposite sex.

GUIDELINES TO HAVING HEALTHY FRIENDSHIPS

1. Do not expect your friend to be responsible for your happiness.

Being happy is your own job and you are the only person that can do it. Too often friendships fail because someone is unhappy and blames their friend for making them feel that way. You need to understand that it is only God who can be your source of continuous joy and happiness. Your friend does not even have the capacity, with all the good intentions in the world, to be your source of fulfilment in life.

Philippians 4:6-7 (NKJV) - *Be anxious for nothing, but in everything by prayer and supplication, with thanksgiving, let your requests be made known to God; and the peace of God, which surpasses all understanding, will guard your hearts and minds through Christ Jesus.*

2. **Do not do anything for your friend if it is based on your expectation that they will have to reciprocate.**

The things you do for your friend must always be done because you chose to do them and you wanted to do them. Do not hold your "good deeds" over their head at a later time.

For example, buying lunch for a woman does not mean she should return the favour by sleeping with you. Paying someone's school fees does not mean he or she should say yes if you choose to propose later. Sponsoring does not give you ownership of anyone!

3. *Be truthful with your friend.*

Many people are taught to lie to protect feelings, either their own or those of their friend.

Colossians 3:9 (NKJV) - *Do not lie to one another, since you have put off the old man with his deeds.*

> Lies create disconnection in friendship, even if your friend never finds out about it.

Proverbs 27:6 (NKJV) - *Faithful are the wounds of a friend, But the kisses of an enemy are deceitful.*

4. Learn to forgive the friend when there is an offence.

Forgiveness is a process of ending your anger or resentment towards another individual. It can have the power to transcend all offenses, great and small, and learning to forgive another takes patience, honesty, and respect. When sincerely given freely in a friendship, forgiveness may heal friendships that are suffering. Forgiveness is an act of humility, not one of haughty feelings.

Colossians 3:13 (NKJV) - Bearing with one another, and forgiving one another, if anyone has a complaint against another; even as Christ forgave you, so you also must do.

5. Be a man or woman of your word.

For example, if you say you're going to meet your friend for lunch at noon, be on time, or call if you're going to be late. Be true to your word and develop faithfulness by keeping your promises and being open.

Proverbs 25:19 (NKJV) - Confidence in an unfaithful man in time of trouble is like a bad tooth and a foot out of joint.

6. Take responsibility for your own actions. Resist the temptation to blame the other for your motives or actions.

The only way to grow or benefit from a friendship is to take responsibility for your actions.

7. Approach your friendship as a learning experience.

We are sometimes attracted to the friend with whom we can learn the most. It is important to know that there are times when some friends come into our life for a season to enable us learn some lessons in life. Some of these friends may not even be around for a long period but they have their use. A truly healthy friendship will consist of both friends who are interested in learning and improving on themselves as well as the friendship.

Proverbs 13:20 (NKJV) - *He who walks with wise men will be wise, But the companion of fools will be destroyed.*

8. Have realistic expectation of your friendship – it will not solve all your problems, only God can!

One person cannot be everything to you. Everybody needs love, intimacy, affection, and affirmation, but your friend alone cannot give you all of that. You need to get some from your friends, from your family, but first and foremost, love God and love yourself.

Psalms 118:8 (NKJV) - *It is better to trust in the Lord Than to put confidence in man.*

For the Christian man or woman, these friendships are critical because they can contribute significantly to our development. They will help us to develop those areas of our lives which formal education or even by just being in church would otherwise not have been necessarily developed.

WHY ARE HEALTHY FRIENDSHIPS SO IMPORTANT?

1. Healthy friendships help us develop emotionally.

Proverbs 27:17 (AMP) - *Iron sharpens iron; so a man sharpens the countenance of his friend [to show rage or worthy purpose].*

Through these friendships we start to learn how to deal with disagreements and anger in general. It is always unfortunate to come across Christian men who raise their fists against women, whenever there is a disagreement or anger. This, if I may boldly say so, is a sign of emotional immaturity and should not be condoned or explained away.

2. Healthy friendships also help us develop intellectually.

Proverbs 13:20 (NKJV) - *He who walks with wise men will be wise, But the companion of fools will be destroyed.*

Do not limit all your knowledge to what you are capable of reading yourself. Healthy friendships can add to your knowledge, and friendships with the opposite sex will give you different perspectives to issues you may not have considered.

3. Healthy friendships also help us develop socially.

Proverbs 18:24 (NKJV) - *A man who has friends must himself be friendly, but there is a friend who sticks closer than a brother.*

You cannot develop social skills just by praying — healthy friendships will teach you.

Every now and then you come across a young man or woman who unfortunately has become so 'spiritual' (so they think) that they are of no earthly value; they do not see the essence of being friendly. It is a deficit that needs to be addressed before such a person starts looking for relationships that may lead to marriage.

These skills include the ability to be civil even with those you disagree with, the ability to listen, as well as how to express yourself without necessarily being aggressive.

4. Healthy friendships also help us to develop morally.

1 Corinthians 15:33 (NKJV) - *Do not be deceived: "Evil company corrupts good habits."*

Proverbs 27:6 (NKJV - *Faithful are the wounds of a friend, but the kisses of an enemy are deceitful.*

For example, a Christian man ought to be able to develop a friendship with a Christian woman without having to sleep with her. You should have friends who can look you in the face and rebuke you if you take the wrong steps, and you will still keep them as friends instead of finding excuses to avoid them from then on.

What do you see as the major challenges to maintaining healthy friendships with the opposite sex?

_____

_____

_____

_____

How much, would you say, friendships with the opposite sex have contributed to your life?

_____

_____

_____

_____

Identify three signs of a healthy friendship and explain how you have seen them at work in your own friendships.

_____

_____

_____

_____

#2
LAYING A SOLID FOUNDATION

Having argued that there is a need for Christian singles to develop friendships with no strings attached, it must also be acknowledged that some of these healthy friendships do sometimes develop into some form or romantic relationships, dating, courtships and eventually marriage.

The Christian single should not therefore develop the attitude that, if even they desire to get married in the future, there is no need to do anything about it now until their 'knight in shining armour' shows up. This very attitude has sometimes led to difficult courtships and unnecessary heartaches.

Contrary to popular belief, the search does not start with going out to look for the so-called Mr. or Miss Right (more about that in the next chapter). It starts with you!

The major secret behind finding Mr. or Miss Right is being a Mr. or Miss Right yourself!

That is it! There is no magic formula per se – it starts with you. If you lay a solid foundation, there is hope that what you build upon it will be stable. No amount of prayer or anointing will sustain what is built on a weak foundation.

Psalms 11:3 (KJV) - *If the foundations be destroyed, what can the righteous do?*

Becoming a 'Mr. or Miss Right' is not an event but a process we all have to go through. It is a continuous process of development because the best 'Mr. Right' can never be a 'Mr. Perfect' in any case.

This development is necessary for every man or woman because one does not go through these steps we are about to look at in order to prepare for marriage, but for life. Marriage in itself is just one of the stations in life – it is not a destination, contrary to what some Christians and teachers have made us believe. Getting married is great but it is not an end in itself. In fact, it is the beginning of another phase of one's life.

For everyone reading this, it is important for you to note that developing yourself is not optional. It is mandatory.

You should not make the mistake of putting your life on hold as a single person holding on to popular statements like:

> ∞ I cannot be whole until I find my 'other half'

> ∞ Marriage will make up for all my weaknesses. (It will actually expose them!)

> ∞ Marriage will meet all my needs

There are three key aspects of this foundation that we all need to develop in order to build for the future.

YOUR VERTICAL RELATIONSHIPS

This basically represents your relationship with God. This relationship should not just be a nominal and religious one. It should be a practical one if it is going to benefit you.

∝ **Develop a strong passion for God – not a half-hearted approach.**

Matthew 22:36-37 (NKJV) - *"Teacher, which is the great commandment in the law?" Jesus said to him, "'You shall love the Lord your God with all your heart, with all your soul, and with all your mind.'*

You should desire to know God for who He is, not just because of what He or someone has promised you. Seek His presence and His blessings will follow.

Matthew 6:33 (NKJV) - *But seek first the kingdom of God and His righteousness, and all these things shall be added to you.*

∝ **Fall in love with God's word and obey it.**

Joshua 1:8 (NKJV) - *This Book of the Law shall not depart from your mouth, but you shall meditate in it day and night, that you may observe to do according to all that is written in it. For then you will make your way prosperous, and then you will have good success.*

Psalms 1:1-3 (NKJV) - *Blessed is the man Who walks not in the counsel of the ungodly, Nor stands in the path of sinners, Nor sits in the seat of the scornful; But his delight is in the law of the Lord, and in His law he meditates day and night. He shall be like a tree planted by the* rivers of water, that brings forth its fruit in its season, Whose leaf also shall not wither; And whatever he does shall prosper.

❦ **Allow God's word to redefine your values in life.**

1 Peter 2:1-2 (NKJV) - *Therefore, laying aside all malice, all deceit, hypocrisy, envy, and all evil speaking, as newborn babes, desire the pure milk of the word, that you may grow thereby.*

Psalms 119:11 (NKJV) - *Your word I have hidden in my heart, That I might not sin against You!*

YOUR HORIZONTAL RELATIONSHIPS

This is where our relationships with others come into play. It is a very important part of the foundation such that if you want to have an idea of who a person is, you will benefit greatly if you study their relationship with people around them.

In this area you learn to do the following:-

❦ **Loving others**

1 John 4:7-8 (NKJV) - *Beloved, let us love one another, for love is of God; and everyone who loves is born of God and knows God. He who does not love does not know God, for God is love.*

❦ **Developing a social life**

Proverbs 18:24 (NKJV) - *A man who has friends must himself be friendly, But there is a friend who sticks closer than a brother.*

A person who has no friends at all will find it difficult, almost impossible to sustain a marriage in future.

❧ *Developing healthy friendships with the opposite gender*

A lot has already been said about healthy friendships in the previous chapter. In order to achieve a more rounded development in this area, you should be able to relate to:-

⇨ Co-equals of the opposite sex

⇨ Superiors of the opposite sex

⇨ Subordinates of the opposite sex

YOUR INTERNAL RELATIONSHIPS

This aspect deals with your relationship with yourself. How one sees one's self goes a long way to affect how one relates to others. You can only love others as much as you love yourself.

> *Mark 12:31 (NKJV) - And the second, like it, is this: 'You shall love your neighbor as yourself.' There is no other commandment greater than these.*

If you cannot stand to be with yourself, what makes you think others would?

When you love yourself, you do the following:

❧ *Have a vision for your life*

> *Proverbs 29:18 (KJV) - Where there is no vision, the people perish: but he that keepeth the law, happy is he.*

> *Habakkuk 2:2 (KJV) - And the LORD answered me, and said, Write the vision, and make it plain upon tables, that he may run that readeth it.*

God gave Adam an assignment before He gave him a companion and helper.

❧ *Fall in love with knowledge and wisdom*

Proverbs 3:13-15 (NKJV) - *Happy is the man who finds wisdom, and the man who gains understanding; for her proceeds are better than the profits of silver, and her gain than fine gold. She is more precious than rubies, And all the things you may desire cannot compare with her.*

> **A man without an assignment has no business looking for a helper.**

Proverbs 4:7 (NKJV) - *Wisdom is the principal thing; Therefore get wisdom. And in all your getting, get understanding.*

Have a good appetite for educative material. Read wide to develop yourself – both formally and informally.

❧ *Develop a healthy self-esteem*

See yourself the way God sees you. Don't compromise or devalue yourself.

1 Corinthians 3:16-17 (NKJV) - *Do you not know that you are the temple of God and that the Spirit of God dwells in you? If anyone defiles the temple of God, God will destroy him. For the temple of God is holy, which temple you are.*

This chapter mentions 'vertical relationships'. How do you see this type of relationship helping you when it comes to a key relationship like marriage?

_____

_____

_____

_____

List three benefits that one can derive from having strong and healthy 'horizontal relationships'.

_____

_____

_____

_____

What does this statement mean to you? "If you cannot stand to be with yourself, what makes you think others would?"

_____

_____

_____

_____

.

#3
THE SEARCH BEGINS (FINDING MR. OR MISS RIGHT)

Now that we've dealt with the laying of the foundation in the previous chapter, our attention now shifts to the other person who we will choose to spend the rest of our lives with, when the opportunity avails itself.

We need to understand a few basic truths before we embark on this journey. Firstly, you are unique. There really is none like you so don't frustrate yourself looking for someone exactly like you. You will go a full circle and end up with yourself!

Secondly, differences are not always negative so the fact that someone may do something differently from what you are used to does not necessary mean they are wrong. Yes, we all have our preferences but unless something is contrary to God's word, you shouldn't reject people at the first instance of anything that is different from what you are used to.

Thirdly, you can only really change one person in your marriage and that person is you! If you start off on a mission to change the person you choose, you may set yourself up for a lifetime of frustration.

Fourthly, this is arguably the most important choice you will be making. You don't get to choose your parents or siblings but you get to choose your spouse.

Let's now look at a biblical example of the search for a life partner although the cultural context may be different for most 21st century Christians like us.

Genesis 24:1-20 (NKJV) - Now Abraham was old, well advanced in age; and the Lord had blessed Abraham in all things. So Abraham said to the oldest servant of his house, who ruled over all that he had, "Please, put your hand under my thigh, and I will make you swear by the Lord, the God of heaven and the God of the earth, that you will not take a wife for my son from the daughters of the Canaanites, among whom I dwell; but you shall go to my country and to my family, and take a wife for my son Isaac." And the servant said to him, "Perhaps the woman will not be willing to follow me to this land. Must I take your son back to the land from which you came?" But Abraham said to him, "Beware that you do not take my son back there. The Lord God of heaven, who took me from my father's house and from the land of my family, and who spoke to me and swore to me, saying, 'To your descendants I give this land,' He will send His angel before you, and you shall take a wife for my son from there. And if the woman is not willing to follow you, then you will be released from this oath; only do not take my son back there." So the servant put his hand under the thigh of Abraham his master, and swore to him concerning this matter. Then the servant took ten of his master's camels and departed, for all his master's goods were in his hand. And he arose and went to Mesopotamia, to the city of Nahor. And he made his camels kneel down outside the city by a well of water at evening time, the time when women go out to draw water. Then he said, "O Lord God of my master Abraham, please give me success this day, and show kindness to my master Abraham. Behold, here I stand by the well of water, and the daughters of the men of the city are coming out to draw water. Now let it be that the young woman to whom I say, 'Please let down your pitcher that I may drink,' and she says, 'Drink, and I will also give your camels a drink'--let her be the one You have appointed for Your servant Isaac. And by this I will know that You have shown kindness to my master."And it happened, before he had finished speaking, that behold, Rebekah, who was born to Bethuel, son of Milcah, the wife of Nahor, Abraham's brother, came out with her pitcher on her shoulder. Now the young woman was very beautiful to behold, a virgin; no man had known her. And she went down to the well, filled her pitcher, and came up. And the servant ran to meet her and said, "Please let me drink a little water from your pitcher." So she said, "Drink, my lord." Then she quickly let her pitcher down to her hand, and gave him a drink. And when she had finished giving him a drink, she said, "I will draw water for your camels also, until they have finished drinking." Then she quickly emptied her pitcher into the trough, ran back to the well to draw water, and drew for all his camels.

In the above account, we read of Abraham sending the oldest servant of his house to look for a wife for his son Isaac. Abraham gave his servant specific instructions as to where to go for Isaac's wife. Abraham was not just looking for a wife for Isaac. He had a criterion.

Genesis 24:3-4 (NKJV) - And I will make you swear by the Lord, the God of heaven and the God of the earth, that you will not take a wife for my son from the daughters of the Canaanites, among whom I dwell; but you shall go to my country and to my family, and take a wife for my son Isaac."

Firstly, Abraham was adamant that the wife should not be a Canaanite, but that the servant should go back to Abraham's country for a wife. This is not a basis for which a New Testament Christian should

31

declare that they will only marry from their tribe or country.

The Canaanites were idol worshippers and God had warned Abraham not to marry from there or else they were going to turn their hearts away from worshipping the Lord God.

Secondly, the servant raised an important question of what was to happen if the newly-found wife was not prepared to relocate to the land of Canaan. He wanted to know if Isaac could be sent there instead.

Genesis 24:4-8 (NKJV) - but you shall go to my country and to my family, and take a wife for my son Isaac." And the servant said to him, "Perhaps the woman will not be willing to follow me to this land. Must I take your son back to the land from which you came?" **But Abraham said to him, "Beware that you do not take my son back there.** *The Lord God of heaven, who took me from my father's house and from*

How often have fruitful, vibrant Christians walked out of bible-believing churches and sometimes even from the faith in search of a spouse!

the land of my family, and who spoke to me and swore to me, saying, 'To your descendants I give this land,' He will send His angel before you, and you shall take a wife for my son from there. **And if the woman is not willing to follow you, then you will be released from this oath; only do not take my son back there."**

In addition to not wanting a wife from Canaan, Abraham was not ready for Isaac to move back to his country in order to find a wife. He went further to explain that the land of Canaan had been promised them by God and so he was not prepared to send his son Isaac out of the

Promised Land in search of a wife! He was prepared to cancel the whole search for a wife if it was going to compromise Isaac's stay in the Promised Land. He repeated the statement '*only do not take my son back there*'.

The process of finding a mate and getting married, as exciting as it may be, should not put us in a position where we are ready to compromise the will of God in order to achieve it.

If you want to get married at all cost, you will later find out that you haven't got what it takes to pay the price of your desperation.

Thirdly, the servant also added to the criteria. He believed God for a wife who was ready to go the extra mile in being hospitable even to a total stranger. A wife who had the presence of mind to realize that the thirsty man who was accompanied by camel would also like to have water for his camel, without him asking.

> *Genesis 24:12-14 (NKJV)* - *Then he said, "O Lord God of my master Abraham, please give me success this day, and show kindness to my master Abraham. Behold, here I stand by the well of water, and the daughters of the men of the city are coming out to draw water. Now let it be that the young woman to whom I say, 'Please let down your pitcher that I may drink,' and she says, 'Drink, and I will also give your camels a drink'--let her be the one You have appointed for Your servant Isaac. And by this I will know that You have shown kindness to my master."*

So we see clearly that even the cultural context in which Abraham was choosing a wife for his son had a criterion.

Some have questioned the relevance of this whole criteria business. Do we really need one? Surely, God can point one out and all our problems will be solved? Well, God gave us the power of choice and alongside with prayer we have to use that power to make the ultimate choice.

Now the big question: Which of these will you like to perform an open heart surgery on you?

ଔ A regular cocaine user

ଔ A psychopathic murderer

ଔ A medical graduate who cheated his way through medical school

Do I hear you asking, where is the "None of the Above" option? Why are you not considering choosing any of them? Surely, all of them have their uses. For example, if you want to do some drug deals I am sure the cocaine user will be a very helpful contact. If you are looking for a contract killer, the murderer has the requisite experience. The dodgy medical graduate will definitely be a master at any fraudulent activity, I guess.

So they all have their uses but it is vital that you know what position you are recruiting for, before you select a suitable candidate. Often, people have chosen a candidate and tried to convince everyone around them, after they've convinced themselves that the person will fit the position of a marriage partner.

I humbly suggest that this has been one of the reasons why a lot of marriages fail at the very early stages — even in the church.

So what is this marriage partner position that we are recruiting for?

Firstly, God sees marriage as a covenant — not just a covenant but one of which He Himself is a witness.

Malachi 2:14 (NKJV) - Yet you say, "For what reason?" Because **the Lord has been witness between you and the wife of your youth,** *With whom you have dealt treacherously; Yet she is your companion* **And your wife by covenant.**

> **Trust is the currency of the marriage covenant. Never think that you can successfully marry someone you cannot trust.**

The marriage covenant is a binding and solemn agreement sealed by vows. It is also a divine arrangement based on trust and commitment.

It therefore requires an unconditional commitment to each other and it is a relationship which should be marked by mutual self-sacrifice.

You are going to be doing the following with the person with whom you enter this covenant called marriage:-

Sacrifice – putting the person's needs above yours.

Sharing – sharing everything with the person including your wealth, debt, friends, enemies and body as well.

Security – you will protect the person. So, for example, if the person you have chosen to enter this covenant with is one who indulges in some illegal activities, you will soon find yourself having to protect him or her and their activities.

Companionship – you will build and maintain a lifetime friendship with the person.

This should give you a fair idea of how much of an impact that choice will make on the rest of your lives.

Now that you know the position you are recruiting for, you can start working on your criteria and approach.

You often hear the question — what do you want in a life partner? This is sometimes followed by a long list of all sorts of interesting attributes from the sublime to the ridiculous.

YOUR CRITERIA

We all tend to have attributes of the ideal person; attributes which almost every married person will tell you are almost always non-attainable. However, you should have your 'negotiables' and 'non-negotiables' columns.

Your 'non-negotiable's are things which you are not ready to compromise on under any circumstances. The general rules for the 'non-negotiables' are those which bother on the spiritual state of the "ideal person". (You need to know whether they are born-again or not.) Their core values are also non-negotiable.

ᔆ *The spiritual state of the person is a matter of eternal consequence. You cannot risk that!*

This is a non-negotiable because of what the scripture tells us in:-

2 Corinthians 6:14-15 (NKJV) - Do not be unequally yoked together with unbelievers. For what fellowship has righteousness with lawlessness? And what communion has light with darkness? And what accord has Christ with Belial? Or what part has a believer with an unbeliever?

What part has a believer with an unbeliever? This is a spiritual reality that will affect your life. As such you should not complain when he decides to interfere because he has control over 50% of your marriage – your spouse.

> **If you marry an unbeliever, you end up with the Devil as your spiritual father-in-law.**

Your children will also find themselves in a situation where they are brought up by possibly, two sets of values.

As pastors, we like to sound a note of caution to young born-again women especially, who knowingly marry unbelievers and later start to stress the gentlemen out about becoming Christians. They are likely to rebel. It even gets more complicated when the children start growing and Mummy is saying one thing and Daddy is saying and doing exactly the opposite. Mummy says do not drink alcohol. Meanwhile, Daddy calls his son to clear up after his regular drinking sessions and laughs when he catches his son sipping the leftovers whilst clearing the table. That is when most of these frustrated wives start calling their husbands 'devils'!

ଓ *The core values of the person determine what he or she will do when there is no one watching. The core values determine the real person, not his or her performance.*

Your 'negotiables' are those things which can be worked on, but even if they do not change or improve, you are still capable of living with. These are also things that can be worked on without the outcome adversely affecting the relationship.

Aspects such as physical appearance and level of wealth could be 'negotiable'. These have been known to change in most relationships although a person who is poor and may seem very comfortable with his or her situation, and who is not ready to learn new things to improve his or her situation will not take you very far!

We will address the criteria in greater detail in the next chapter.

YOUR APPROACH

Over the years I have heard of many strange and interesting ways in which people have sought to secure a partner with the intent of spending the rest of their lives together. Some approaches are well-thought out whilst others can only be termed rather 'reckless'.

I cannot leave this subject without sharing this case with you. A female friend goes for an appointment with her cardiologist and whilst sitting in the waiting room, a gentleman walks past briefly and then suddenly returns with this note for the lady:

Dear Madam,

Application for Employment

I wish to be considered for the position of Manager of your heart with the following job description:

⇨ *Take care of your heart*

⇨ *Hold your heart*

⇨ *Touch your heart*

⇨ *Protect your heart*

⇨ *Take absolute control*

Some may call this love at first sight, but these borders on the ridiculous and can land you in major trouble!

There are mainly four pillars that should define your approach.

PILLAR 1: IT TAKES ONE TO KNOW ONE

Build yourself up in the areas that you are looking for in others. If you desire to spend your life with someone who is astute in business and financial markets, you should also know at least something about the area.

You shouldn't be the kind who thinks stock market is a place where they sell stock fish or that the FTSE is a four-footed monster. It is a shame that so many require of their future life partners what they are not prepared to become.

If you are not a godly man, why are you looking for a godly woman? It is the godliness in you that will attract that same quality in them.

Build up in the areas where you know you are lacking. For example, if you know you have a problem with your temper, you start working on your anger management techniques to make you a better person.

PILLAR 2: TRUST GOD TO LEAD YOU IN YOUR CHOICE

> ***Proverbs 3:5-6 (NKJV)*** *- Trust in the Lord with all your heart, And lean not on your own understanding; In all your ways acknowledge Him, And He shall direct your paths.*

Pray before you get to the point where you become emotionally involved with someone because then you are tempted to ask God to rubber stamp your choice.

You have to trust God to lead you in the choice of the person that you want to get married to because feelings are very transient. One day, your feelings tell you that that person is so nice and the next day the same person is not as attractive.

Committing it to God in prayer and having the peace of God about your decision to go ahead is very important. This is because if you go through this experience, you develop a strong conviction that this is the person God wants me to be with, and it goes a long way to help you commit to making the relationship work.

Know yourself – be bold enough to admit when your flesh is leading you instead of God.

Have you noticed how in almost every Christian group, the attractive looking girls are always having scores of men who have 'heard from God' concerning them? Doesn't God know the other girls in the same group?

It is important to be honest with yourself, so that you can admit it when you know your flesh is talking to you about someone.

PILLAR 3: DON'T GAMBLE WITH YOUR SPIRITUAL WELL-BEING

Your faith will go beyond your feeling. Your faith will ultimately determine the safe boundaries of your marriage.

Remember, it is your faith that will keep you going during the days when your feelings are not that great.

Your faith will determine the environment in which your children will grow.

Ladies, the one you choose will be your spiritual head whether you like it or not. Are they qualified?

The same person who said he or she doesn't have a problem with you going to church will one day expect you to be at the social gatherings he or she organizes on Sundays, during the period you otherwise should have been in church!

If you are happy with choosing them when they are not going to church, don't expect to force them to church after you marry them.

PILLAR 4: FOCUS ON CHARACTER TRAITS

Integrity – What is the value of this person's word? Can you trust them? Are they truthful?

Humility – there is no future for anyone who is not ready to learn in life. Pride comes before a fall.

Flexibility – if they cannot adapt, they will not make it with you in the future. How do they respond to change?

Response to Authority – if he cannot respect the role of the church and the Pastor in your life, note that if you one day run into problems, there will be no one to draw the line in your life.

#3 – STUDY GUIDE

In Gen 24:1-20, we read of Abraham seeking a wife for his son, Isaac. Apart from the idea of a father choosing a bride for his son, which is very foreign to most modern day cultures, what are some of the other lessons that can be learnt from his approach?

_____

_____

_____

_____

According to this chapter, what are the four key responsibilities you have towards the person with whom you enter the marriage covenant?

_____

_____

_____

_____

Once a prospective partner is born-again, there is no need to focus on examining that person's character traits. Discuss

_____

_____

_____

_____

#4
CHOOSING A PARTNER FOR LIFE NOT STRIFE

The obvious question that springs to mind once anyone hears this title is, "Why would any sound person deliberately choose a partner for strife?" Well, you may be hard-pressed to find anyone who goes out there purposefully to do so, but quite a lot of people end up doing exactly that because of what they look out for, what they miss and in some cases what they consciously disregard during their courtship.

For example, although a person may not deliberately go out there looking for frustration, I am sure you will agree with me that the person who goes out to purchase a used mobile phone that is already ten years old (if you can find one!) and of some unknown brand is setting themselves up for a life of frustration. This will happen to this person simply because of what that person may choose to disregard in making their decision to purchase.

Courtship is almost an old-fashioned word now but it is that phase in a relationship where two parties have clearly expressed their intention to marry each other. At this stage, the relationship moves as closest to marriage as possible.

Courtship can be exciting, and once again there is the need for us to know some ground rules, to enable us to get the maximum benefit from it.

❧ COURTSHIP IS AN OPPORTUNITY FOR THE PROSPECTIVE COUPLE TO STUDY EACH OTHER

This stage of the relationship provides you a great opportunity to get to know more about each other before you make the final move into marriage. However, some have missed this opportunity by spending most of their courtship in publicly showing themselves off wherever they go, and busily acting 'husband and wife'.

> We sometimes forget that how other people view our relationship is not half as important as the real state of the relationship.

❧ COURTSHIP IS NOT A MERE FORMALITY. IT IS YOUR OPPORTUNITY TO BUILD A STRONG FOUNDATION FOR THE FUTURE MARRIAGE, IF ANY

Most people assume that every courtship eventually ends in marriage and as a result of that we tend to think it is just a formality for us to go through, so as to satisfy our church's requirements, if any, and get married. We hang on to statements like 'as long as we love each other, we will be alright'; 'love is the only thing required for a successful marriage.' Courtship is actually a very serious phase of our relationship and we should treat it with the seriousness it deserves, and learn as much as we can about how to make the relationship and perhaps the marriage, one that God desires, during that period.

> *Proverbs 24:3-4 (NKJV) - Through wisdom a house is built, and by understanding it is established; by knowledge the rooms are filled with all precious and pleasant riches.*

❧ COURTSHIP IS NOT MARRIAGE AND SHOULD NOT BE TREATED AS SUCH

As straight-forward as this may sound, many have gone into courtship with the mindset that once they are in a courtship, they've committed their future to the relationship so there is only one possible outcome – marriage.

This has accounted for some disastrous marriages in some cases, because obvious major problems were overlooked right during the courtship stage.

This has also sometimes led to courtships where parties act as if they own each other and it results in very difficult and unhappy courtships, which if not dealt with will graduate into miserable marriages.

❧ A BROKEN COURTSHIP IS ALWAYS BETTER THAN A BROKEN MARRIAGE

Many Christians tend to believe that a broken courtship is a disaster. Of course, there cannot be a broken courtship without hurt and disappointment. However, we have to be conscious of the fact that courtships have two possible outcomes – marriage or decision not to proceed to marry each other. None of these outcomes should be considered as disasters.

> In fact, some courtships, if properly run, should end in a decision not to proceed to marriage!

This is one key reason why it is important to have respect for each other's bodies during courtship so that if it doesn't end up in marriage, the individuals involved do not end up feeling used and rejected.

I dare say, there are some married people out there now who will be nodding in agreement as well as regret, secretly, as they read this.

❧ THE LENGTH OF THE COURTSHIP DOES NOT GUARANTEE ITS QUALITY

As much as very short courtships (less than six months) do not give the couple enough time to learn much about each other, in my opinion, having very long courtships (four years and in some cases, more) does not guarantee its quality either.

What matters is what one does during that period, which we will be looking at shortly. These long courtships are sometimes fraught with problems – frustration, compromises and a lot of hurts when one person decides to walk away after the period.

25 QUESTIONS YOU SHOULD BE ANSWERING DURING COURTSHIP

1. HAS THERE BEEN A MARRIAGE PROPOSAL IN THIS RELATIONSHIP?

It is absolutely necessary for courtship to have a clear proposal and an acceptance. The absence of these can lead to dangerous assumptions.

For example, there are cases where one person thinks she is in courtship with a gentleman who hasn't actually proposed, and is actually 'enjoying the ride'. However, he being a smooth talker keeps saying nice things to the lady – 'whenever I see you, I am happy' etc. She is thinking this is nice and special so the next day she gets close to him just in case he will release another one of his 'specials'. Being gifted in that department, the gentleman doesn't let her down and unleashes another and she keeps drawing closer and closer in hope. One day, the gentleman comes to her, smiling, with a testimony. "Mary, guess what! I have found my life partner and thought I should let you know since you are such a special friend". Mary takes off to her house and collapses in a pool of tears. Later, she is in her pastor's office and the pastor doesn't know whether to rejoice or be angry when the gentleman comes in later to share his 'testimony' with the pastor. His reaction when the pastor asks him about Mary is simple and almost dismissive – "she was a good friend and I never thought of her that way. She was like a sister".

2. HAS THE MARRIAGE PROPOSAL BEEN ACCEPTED?

Do not assume that a proposal has been accepted just because the person you proposed to is still being nice to you and in some cases, even going out on dates with you! You may end up making major commitments to this relationship only for your world to be shattered when the other person eventually disengages.

3. WHAT ARE MY PARTNER'S BELIEFS?

What a person believes forms a very vital part of their lives. If you are considering to enter into the marriage covenant with someone (as already explained in a previous chapter), you better make sure you are all going in the same direction or you will be choosing for strife!

Amos 3:3 (NKJV) - Can two walk together, unless they are agreed?

4. WHAT ARE MY PARTNER'S VALUES?

A person's core values will determine what they will do when no one is watching. It determines the kind of boundaries they will willingly place around their lives. Their values determine who they really are. The person may be going to church as a habit but their values will determine the extent to which the Christian teachings they are exposed to become part of their lives.

5. IS MY PARTNER GENUINELY BORN-AGAIN?

This issue has come up time and time again whenever the subject of the choice of marriage partners comes up. Many Pastors and churches have had to grapple with it and Christians have had to deal with the issue of so-called success stories when people of different faiths are portrayed as having successful marriages. Some Christians have used these examples as the basis for their decision to marry those who are not born-again. Firstly, what does the Bible say?

> *2 Corinthians 6:14-15 (NKJV)* - *Do not be unequally yoked together with unbelievers. For what fellowship has righteousness with lawlessness? And what communion has light with darkness? And what accord has Christ with Belial? Or what part has a believer with an unbeliever?*

We cannot deny the fact that Paul frowns on this. Secondly, those who try to ignore this scripture and defy counsel to marry those Paul refers to as unbelievers sometimes forget that the issue also comes up when you start raising children.

6. DOES MY PARTNER HAVE INTEGRITY?

How much of your partner's word can you actually rely on? Can you trust this person or do you have to double-check everything he or she says or does, before you can accept it?

Proverbs 25:19 (NKJV) *- Confidence in an unfaithful man in time of trouble Is like a bad tooth and a foot out of joint.*

You really have no business entering a marriage covenant with someone you simply cannot trust. You will be setting yourself up for a life of frustration.

7. HOW DOES MY PARTNER REACT TO VICTORY?

Does this person know how to celebrate his or her victories gracefully? Or does he or she have to put you down anytime they win, before they can enjoy their victory? Those who cannot celebrate gracefully may pose problems in the future when they chalk personal successes later on in life. There have been several instances of successful wives who suddenly disregard their husbands, and successful husbands who shun their wives because they feel they've made it in life.

8. HOW DOES MY PARTNER REACT TO DEFEAT?

How do they react when they lose? Do they find out why and how and want to win later? Do they coil into their shell and start to feel sorry for themselves? Do they blame everyone else around them? Are they simply very bad losers? Do they sulk and refuse to talk to anyone after losing?

Be careful when dealing with people who tend to be very bad losers because they normally do not handle other peoples' successes very well. They feel intimidated and they react in ways which can make married life with them tortuous.

9. HOW PREPARED IS MY PARTNER TO LEARN FROM OTHERS?

It is good to marry someone who has strong opinions and know how to work with them, but someone who is not prepared to learn from anyone else is a walking time bomb. Remember, you will most likely be closest to them when they explode!

> *Proverbs 4:7-9 (NKJV)* - *Wisdom is the principal thing; Therefore get wisdom. And in all your getting, get understanding. 8 Exalt her, and she will promote you; She will bring you honor, when you embrace her. She will place on your head an ornament of grace; A crown of glory she will deliver to you.*

> *Proverbs 13:20 (NKJV)* - *He who walks with wise men will be wise, but the companion of fools will be destroyed.*

10. HOW DOES MY PARTNER REACT TO LACK?

Is my partner prepared to live within his or her means or will he or she break any rule in order to get out of lack? Whereas you should not be satisfied with someone who doesn't seem prepared to lift a finger even when they are staring at starvation, you should also be looking for the ability of the person to be content with where they are now, whilst working on a way out.

> *Philippians 4:12 (NKJV)* - *I know how to be abased, and I know how to abound. Everywhere and in all things I have learned both to be full and to be hungry, both to abound and to suffer need.*

11. HOW DOES MY PARTNER REACT TO ABUNDANCE?

Does my partner see abundance as the ultimate to achieve in life or the means to make him or her more effective? Is he or she selfless? Does he or she lose their sense of judgment during times like these? There are those who've suffered from this last tendency so badly that they walk away from church once they see a measure of financial increase in their lives.

> *Luke 12:19-20 (NKJV) - And I will say to my soul, "Soul, you have many goods laid up for many years; take your ease; eat, drink, and be merry." 'But God said to him, 'Fool! This night your soul will be required of you; then whose will those things be which you have provided?'*

12. IS MY PARTNER DILIGENT?

> *Proverbs 10:26 (NKJV) - As vinegar to the teeth and smoke to the eyes, So is the lazy man to those who send him.*

Marrying someone who is lazy can set you on a path to lifetime misery and frustration.

13. HOW DOES MY PARTNER RELATE TO THEIR OWN FAMILY?

How your partner treats his or her own family may be an indication of what lies ahead of you. A person who has issues with every single member of his or her family should raise question marks in your mind.

> *Ephesians 6:2-3 (NKJV) - "Honor your father and mother," which is the first commandment with promise: "that it may be well with you and you may live long on the earth."*

14. WHAT KIND OF FRIENDS DOES MY PARTNER HAVE?

One cannot choose your parents or siblings but your friends are ones you choose. The calibre of a person's friends is therefore a good indication of their sense of judgment.

> ***Proverbs 28:7 (NKJV)*** - *Whoever keeps the law is a discerning son, but a companion of gluttons shames his father.*

> ***Proverbs 13:20 (NKJV)*** - *He who walks with wise men will be wise, but the companion of fools will be destroyed.*

15. HOW DOES MY PARTNER RELATE TO MEMBERS OF THE OPPOSITE SEX?

If your partner cannot relate to members of the opposite sex in a pure and honourable way then you are setting yourself up for trouble.

> ***1 Timothy 5:1-2 (NKJV)*** - *Do not rebuke an older man, but exhort him as a father, younger men as brothers, older women as mothers, younger as sisters, with all purity.*

You should not find yourself in a courtship where you are competing with others for the attention of your partner.

Paul admonishes Timothy to treat the younger women with all purity.

16. HAS MY PARTNER CONQUERED PRIDE IN THEIR LIVES?

Choosing a partner who feels he or she is doing you a big favour by marrying you is a recipe for disaster. If your partner feels he or she is 'descending' in order to pick you up from the gutter of life, that partner is going to find it difficult sticking with you during the tough phases of life. Also, if someone with this attitude excels beyond his or her partner, he or she will always put that partner down. If you excel beyond this proud partner, he or she will simply not be able to celebrate you, and that is where you end up in a life of strife.

> *Proverbs 16:18-19 (NKJV)* - *Pride goes before destruction, and a haughty spirit before a fall. Better to be of a humble spirit with the lowly, than to divide the spoil with the proud.*

17. HAS MY PARTNER CONQUERED BITTERNESS IN THEIR LIVES?

Although this may not be a deal-breaker from the beginning, it is something to be addressed urgently. Many courtships have suffered seriously because one or both parties may have had some bitter experiences in the past – either during their childhood days or worse still from previous relationships and associations. One major area in which this manifests is when you have someone who is yet to recover from previous betrayal and simply cannot trust you!

Bitterness defiles our spirit and the earlier one deals with it, through counselling and prayer, the better.

> *Hebrews 12:15 (NKJV)* - *Looking carefully lest anyone fall short of the grace of God; lest any root of bitterness springing up cause trouble, and by this many become defiled;*

18. DOES MY PARTNER RESPECT ME?

This is a question that most people either miss or conveniently dismiss when they are already overcome by their emotional attachment to their partner. As much as that initial excitement of relationships may set your head high up in the clouds, you need to know that one of the key requirements of a biblical and successful marriage is the ability of the husband and wife to honour each other.

I will like to sound a note of warning here that a partner who starts to abuse you verbally or physically whilst in courtship, is bad news – in fact, very bad news, and if that doesn't change very quickly during the courtship, your marriage is most likely to be one full of strife. Instead of finding excuses for the abuser, use your God-given right to get out of that courtship and protect your future.

> *1 Peter 3:7 (NKJV) - Husbands, likewise, dwell with them with understanding, giving honor to the wife, as to the weaker vessel, and as being heirs together of the grace of life, that your prayers may not be hindered.*

19. DOES MY PARTNER HAVE A SENSE OF PURPOSE IN LIFE?

Do you know where your partner is going in life? Or does he himself know where he is heading? This is most important, especially for the women, because if a woman is going to choose someone to be the head of their union, it is only logical that the woman gets to know where the head is heading! Following someone who doesn't know where he or she is going is

> **When you are saddled with too many passengers in life, it affects the speed with which you can progress in life.**

one of the most frustrating and annoying experiences. No wonder this sort of situation always leads to strife. No matter how handsome and polite a man may be, without a sense of purpose, you will be stuck with a great dose of frustration and excuses if you marry him!

For the men as well, it is important you choose women of purpose. Marriage is not a destination; it is the beginning of another phase of your journey. So if the woman's only vision is to get married, then you risk having a perpetual passenger in your vehicle called marriage.

In marital life, you cannot afford to carry passengers forever – both of you have to be able to drive.

> ***Proverbs 4:25-26 (NKJV)*** *- Let your eyes look straight ahead, And your eyelids look right before you. Ponder the path of your feet, and let all your ways be established.*

20. IS MY PARTNER READY TO TAKE RESPONSIBILITY FOR THEIR ACTIONS?

Is my partner the kind of person who is ready to accept responsibility when things go wrong, or an expert at blaming everyone else but themselves for anything that may go wrong in their lives? Does he or she consistently blame the whole world for their actions or inactions?

> ***Proverbs 22:13 (NKJV)*** *- The lazy man says, "There is a lion outside! I shall be slain in the streets!"*

21. CAN I RELATE WELL WITH MY PARTNER SOCIALLY?

Marriage is a lifetime commitment and as such it is important that the person you share your married life with is a person you can develop a healthy friendship with. Companionship is a key element of marriage and when considering this question you should bear in mind that you start your married life with your companion and whether you have children or not, you will spend the final days of this journey with the same person.

22. CAN I RELATE WELL WITH MY PARTNER INTELLECTUALLY?

Although one's intellectual ability cannot be used as the sole criteria for deciding on your partner, a huge gap in your intellectual abilities can ultimately affect the quality of your communication. Most marriage counsellors will bear testimony to the fact that when there is a big gap, you end up with situations where the more intellectual party starts to develop deeply emotional friendships in their circles to the detriment of the marriage. This can result in unhealthy emotional gaps developing in the marriage.

23. CAN I RELATE WELL WITH MY PARTNER SPIRITUALLY?

There is power in the prayer of agreement and this is one of the major tools every marriage should use both to gain spiritual victories and also build the spiritual intimacy.

> *Matthew 18:19-20 (NKJV) - Again I say to you that if two of you agree on earth concerning anything that they ask, it will be done for them by My Father in heaven. For where two or three are gathered together in My name, I am there in the midst of them."*

24. DOES THE AGE DIFFERENCE ALLOW US TO BE COMFORTABLE WITH EACH OTHER'S FOCUS IN LIFE?

The issue of the age difference between spouses has been a subject of many debates over the years but where the difference is fifteen years or more, one should bear in mind that as the years go by there is a tendency that this difference can pose its own set of problems. For example, a 40-year old and a 60-year old are bound to have very different perspectives on life. When a marriage gets to that point, there is a tendency that the couple may just grow apart.

25. DOES THE AGE DIFFERENCE ALLOW US TO BE COMFORTABLE AROUND EACH OTHER'S FRIENDS?

Once again, where there is an age gap of fifteen years or more, one should take into consideration that it will be very difficult to relate well with one's spouse's close friends if they happen to be twenty years older. For example, a 30-year old wife will find it a bit challenging to enjoy the company of the fifty-something year old friends of her husband!

5 KEY QUESTIONS YOU SHOULD BE ABLE TO ANSWER ABOUT A POTENTIAL HUSBAND

ଔ Has he got the ability to lead?

ଔ Does he have a selfless attitude?

ଔ How does he respond to authority?

ଔ Do I like his physical appearance?

ଔ Is he a committed Christian?

5 KEY QUESTIONS YOU SHOULD BE ABLE TO ANSWER ABOUT A POTENTIAL WIFE

ଓ Is she adaptable?

ଓ Does she have a selfless attitude?

ଓ Does she demonstrate a healthy level of independence?

ଓ Do I like her physical appearance?

ଓ Is she a committed Christian?

Out of the 25 questions you should be answering during courtship, which three do you consider the most important and why?

_____

_____

_____

_____

One will inevitably have friends of the opposite sex, even after marriage, so why is it necessary to know how your prospective partner relates in this area?

_____

_____

_____

_____

A broken courtship is always better than a broken marriage'. Discuss

_____

_____

_____

_____

Think Before You Wink

#5
INGREDIENTS OF A SUCCESSFUL COURTSHIP

A lot of the background information about courtship has already been covered in the previous chapter.

Courtship presents a person the opportunity to further study their fiancé or fiancée after they have stated their intention to marry the person.

This period of courtship can be very exciting, as the couple spend time together -thinking and planning the future.

There is a general assertion that a successful courtship is one that ends in marriage. Contrary to this belief, the success of courtship should not be determined by whether or not it results in marriage.

As much as society will love to see all courtships ending up in marriage, some courtships are better off ending in anything but a marriage. Unfortunately, there is this general perception that a courtship which does not end in marriage is a failure.

This has sometimes led to unhealthy marriages and one can argue that bad courtships have contributed to a lot of bad marriages, and hence the increasing divorce rate.

The emotional excitement associated with courtship makes it even more difficult for the partners to be level-headed in their assessment of each other. As a result, most people end up putting more effort in playing 'man and wife' - with public displays of affection instead of consciously learning about each other with the future in mind. For courtship to be successful there are some key ingredients that need to be present and this chapter will deal with these.

LOVE

Courtship gives us the opportunity to demonstrate love to each other and it must not be confused with lust. One of the basic differences between these two is that whilst true loves gives, lust takes, whilst true love cherishes the interest and well-being of the other person, lust focuses on its own self-serving interest. Love reflects the nature of God whereas lust reflects the flesh, and is contrary to God's nature. Love is very key to any courtship because it is one of the key elements that keeps a relationship going when all else fails.

> *1 Corinthians 13:4-7 (NKJV)* - *Love suffers long and is kind; love does not envy; love does not parade itself, is not puffed up; does not behave rudely, does not seek its own, is not provoked, thinks no evil; does not rejoice in iniquity, but rejoices in the truth; bears all things, believes all things, hopes all things, endures all things.*

FORGIVENESS

As long as two people remain in a relationship, they are bound to step on each other's toes at some stage. Courtship is therefore a training ground for the partners to develop the ability to forgive one other when the occasion arises.

Forgiveness is a major key in courtship because where there is no forgiveness the relationship cannot grow. Unforgiveness can also lead to one partner becoming bitter, and in some cases, finding it increasingly difficult to trust the other partner. This does not augur well for the future of the relationship.

> *Colossians 3:12-13 (NKJV)* - *Therefore, as the elect of God, holy and beloved, put on tender mercies, kindness, humility, meekness, longsuffering; bearing with one another, and forgiving one another, if anyone has a complaint against another; even as Christ forgave you, so you also must do.*

TRUST

One of the obstacles that many deal with when it comes to trust is when they have to be in a relationship with a partner who has been hurt or betrayed in a previous relationship. For courtship to negotiate this hurdle successfully, the people involved will need to seek counselling in dealing with the past hurts, so that they can be free to trust again.

A challenging and interesting aspect of trust in relationships is that in any successful relationship, the people involved have to trust each other enough to take each other's word without always having the physical proof! Trust is what makes the average married couple believe each other when they say good bye to each other in the morning with the understanding that they are both heading to their workplaces.

COMMUNICATION

No relationship can survive and grow without good communication. Communication is therefore to be learnt, developed and practiced throughout the courtship. For there to be communication, one needs to be open and frank with their partner. It also requires that the parties involved are honest with each other, even if, what they may be dealing with may not be always easy.

It is important that partners don't allow the overwhelming desire to impress each other to result in them not being transparent with each other.

> ***Colossians 3:9 (NKJV)*** - *Do not lie to one another, since you have put off the old man with his deeds.*

Having said that, it is also important that partners have a lot of light-hearted conversation as it is a great way to develop a friendship.

BOUNDARIES

Since courtship is not yet marriage, it is the sort of relationship that requires partners to have clear boundaries. These boundaries are necessary in two main areas. Firstly, there ought to be clear boundaries as far as their responsibilities to each other are concerned.

Courting couples should not take on responsibilities that are reserved for marriages. For example, it should be clearly understood that a potential husband is not obliged to be the provider for his fiancée whilst in courtship. Whilst in courtship, it is advisable for a couple not to enter contracts such as joint ownership of a house, because it could be very messy if the courtship does not eventually result in marriage.

These boundaries also refer to our sexual behaviour. Simply put, as Christians, we are not to be sexually involved with the person we are not married to.

1 Corinthians 7:1-2 (NKJV) - *Now concerning the things of which you wrote to me: It is good for a man not to touch a woman. Nevertheless, because of sexual immorality, let each man have his own wife, and let each woman have her own husband.*

PLANNING

Most people tend to spend a lot of time together during their courtship for the obvious reason that they are attracted to each other. However, it should not be assumed that all that time is used effectively even if most of the time may be spent talking.

Whereas it is only natural that a courting couple will find time joking and expressing their affection for each other in their conversations, ample time should be dedicated to planning the future.

In planning the future, we are referring to where the individual plans or aspirations of the courting couple are discussed with a view of finding a common ground and working out how both aspirations, if they are very different, will be realized in one way or the other.

This aspect may not sound romantic to some, but that is how you can start laying a solid foundation for your future marriage.

Luke 14:28-30 (NKJV) - *For which of you, intending to build a tower, does not sit down first and count the cost, whether he has enough to finish it-- lest, after he has laid the foundation, and is not able to finish, all who see it begin to mock him, saying, 'This man began to build and was not able to finish.'*

Some very major issues can be totally missed if this practical planning is not done by the couple.

Ken and Grace (not their real names) walked into my office with excitement as they inquired about how soon they could start the premarital counselling.

During the exploratory conversation, I asked Ken what he planned to do after the wedding. He went ahead of to tell me of his detailed plans for travelling abroad for his post-graduate study. There were only two minor problems we discovered that morning – he wasn't quite sure when he intended to return and Grace had no idea of this plan although they were talking about wedding in a matter of a few months!

RELATIONSHIPS

Some people may be surprised about why we are still talking about relationships when we are now at the courtship stage. But this subject is very key at this point.

Firstly, being in courtship does not mean you should suddenly drop all the friends you've had prior to this courtship. In fact, it is not healthy to isolate yourselves from all your friends just because you are now in courtship.

Secondly, this is a good opportunity to start developing some healthy friendships with your fiancé or fiancée's friends. After all, these friends are bound to show up in your lives at some point if you intend to marry this person you are courting.

It is also a perfect opportunity to start studying your partner's friends and relatives because it does provide you with a window into the real life of your partner.

Priscilla (not her real name) was wearing a face of frustration and anger when she narrated to me how her supposedly Christian husband had been spending nights out of the house, sometimes without any reasonable explanation. She went on to tell me about how this husband had been frequenting night clubs.

At this point, I got worried and wondered how this man could have changed so quickly after getting married. Upon further discussion, Priscilla reluctantly revealed that when she first met John, he was frequenting night clubs with his friends so she also joined in so that they could spend time together, although she was then a serious church-going Christian. She had somehow kept that fact away from her church leaders so that their wedding plans would not be disturbed by the nosy leaders.

John was therefore surprised when Priscilla confronted her about the frequent trips to the night club. John and his friends were just living what was a normal life to them and was wondering why Priscilla was suddenly having problems with it. To cut a long story short, they ended up divorcing.

CELEBRATION

The period of courtship is also a time where partners should start cultivating the habit of celebrating each other.

To most people, this may come naturally, as excitement usually runs high during this stage of the relationship. Therefore, if you find yourself in a courtship where your partner simply cannot be bothered when it is your birthday or when you achieve something significant, then something is not quite right.

At this stage, courting couples should learn how to appreciate each other, respect each other's interest and move on to the stage of celebrating their partners. If your partner consistently condemns or demeans your interests and seem to have a clear agenda of 'changing' you when you get married, you will have to resolve this in counselling before you get married or else you will set yourself up for a tough and even miserable marriage.

It is also at this point that you sometimes come across those who are so insecure or selfish that they cannot celebrate their partners if they excel in any way. If a person is always struggling to celebrate you, then he or she cannot appreciate you and as a result, he or she may most likely turn out to be a difficult partner to be with in this journey called marriage.

PRAYER

As Christians, this may sound as though one is stating the obvious but prayer is a much more discussed activity than a practiced one, and the only time we get any benefit out of prayer is when we practice it.

Praying together helps to develop intimacy and once a couple develops this very healthy habit of praying together, it follows on naturally when you move on into marriage.

Praying together about your future plans is not just a ritual. It provokes the blessing of God upon your intended union and fortifies you against any plans the Devil may have for your future home.

> *Proverbs 3:5-6 (NKJV)* - *Trust in the Lord with all your heart, And lean not on your own understanding; In all your ways acknowledge Him, And He shall direct your paths.*

Proverbs 16:3 (NKJV) - *Commit your works to the Lord, And your thoughts will be established.*

UNDERSTANDING

If any marriage counsellor or Pastor were to be paid a dollar whenever they come across a case of a married person complaining about not being understood by their spouse, all Pastors would have been very rich! By this I mean that it is a very common issue.

Courting couples sometimes find it odd when they are told during pre-marital counselling about the importance of building understanding, because most people at that stage simply cannot imagine themselves having any major misunderstanding in their relationships since they are so much in love. Well, reality catches up with them very soon and for some, the shock is simply too much to handle!

Achieving understanding is a very long process and it involves making a conscious effort to learn about your partner, getting to know the differences between the two of you as well as learning to exercise patience with each other.

Learning can be hard work. Please, avoid the temptation of ignoring this aspect, and covering your 'laziness' with statements like 'love conquers all' and 'God is in control!'

Learning these differences can sometimes save us from unnecessary conflicts right from the outset.

Kwame (not his real name) was a very phlegmatic young man who came for pre-marital counselling with Jane (not her real name). After learning about each other's temperaments, he couldn't help but confess that he had been so frustrated by his sanguine fiancée's tendency to talk freely with anybody at any function they attended together, and that he had resorted to warning her anytime they were about to go out, but to no avail. Jane was relieved to hear that the fact that she kept on failing to heed this 'warning' was not because she was rebellious or disrespectful.

Also understanding is what will enable you to live with your spouse in marriage even if he or she does not manage to change what you were wishing to change.

> ***Proverbs 24:3 (NKJV)*** *- Through wisdom a house is built, and by understanding it is established;*

DURATION

There are no stiff and fast rules when it comes to how long the courtship should run for. However, it is important to abide by some guidelines at this stage.

As I have mentioned earlier in this book, one should avoid treating courtship as a mere formality. You should not rush through your courtship just so that you can say you courted before marriage.

I will not advise a courtship to run for less than six months because this will give you some time for the initial excitement to die down a bit so that hopefully, you can see clearly as you study each other. You may have heard the popular statement – 'love is blind'. Well if 'love is blind,' marriage will definitely miraculously restore your sight and for some, they never survive the shock.

On the other hand, one should not 'court' for eternity. A period of 18–24months should be the upper limit. The duration of the courtship alone does not guarantee its quality – it is what really goes on during the courtship that matters.

Indecision should not be allowed to drag a courtship into an unhealthy state where the couple just live together for long periods, and depend on each other like husband and wife. This can sometimes lead to abuse and even if that is not the case, if this type of courtship does not end up in marriage, it leaves one party in a terrible state.

After having courted Dan (not his real name) for almost seven years, Mary, 32years old, had gotten to the point where she considered Dan as her husband, although they hadn't been able to honour any of the wedding dates they fixed over the years. Dan kept postponing it with what appeared to be genuine reasons.

Mary had the shock of her life when she was one day informed by a friend that Dan had just gotten married in the next town and was due to travel abroad. This sent Mary into deep depression and at the age of 44 years, she could still not bring herself to the point of considering a relationship with anyone else!

#5 – STUDY GUIDE

What do you consider to be the five most important ingredients of a successful courtship, out of the entire list given in this chapter and why?

_____

_____

_____

_____

What role does the setting of boundaries play in courtship?

_____

_____

_____

_____

How can friendship with others positively affect your courtship?

_____

_____

_____

_____

#6
STEPPING UP FROM BROKEN COURTSHIPS

Relationships, in general, are wonderful things, and especially when we relate with people we feel comfortable with, we derive a lot of benefits from them.

When we develop affection for someone and start to date the person, we invariably look forward to the relationship growing from mere friendship to a more serious level such as courtship where we notify each other of our intention to spend the rest of our lives with them.

As stated earlier in this book, courtships can be very exciting, especially during the early stages, but it is also important that we stay grounded enough to be able to study each other.

As great as courtship is, there are times when they do not progress according to our expectation and as such do not end up in marriage. This normally brings a lot of disappointment to the people involved. However, it should be noted that a broken courtship is not necessarily the bad news as most of us see it to be.

> A broken courtship is always better than a broken marriage.

The above statement should offer some hope to someone who has had to deal with a broken courtship – it is simply not the end of your life. Failure to appreciate this fact has led to some people holding on to very unhealthy courtships which invariably end up in disastrous marriages.

I will like to firstly address some common myths associated with broken courtships in our society.

7 MYTHS ABOUT BROKEN COURTSHIPS

BROKEN RELATIONSHIPS ARE DISASTERS

There are many who have remained in courtships they should have abandoned, but for the fear of what others may say if they took that decision. What would my friends at church say? Was I not the one who said "God had told me that this man was the one for me"? How will I face my friends and his friends?

It may be great for your friends and relatives to celebrate with you when you announce that you've met someone, but you should always remember that you are the only person who will be living with this choice of yours for the rest of your life.

For example, a courtship that involves physical abuse, sexual abuse or persistent verbal abuse is not a healthy one, and if after persistent efforts to resolve issues through counselling and prayer there are no improvements, it will rather be a disaster to carry on to marriage! Remember once again, a broken courtship is better than a broken marriage.

PEOPLE WHO EXPERIENCE BROKEN COURTSHIPS ARE FAILURES

Yes, there are people who consider those who have been part of broken courtships as failures – they make statements such as, 'she doesn't know how to keep a man', or 'he doesn't know how to treat a woman'.

Well, these may be right in some cases. However, it must also be noted that there are times that courtships have to come to an end because both parties come to the conclusion that they are simply not ready to make the commitment required for marriage to each other. No one should be compelled to marry.

There are also cases where one of the partners' vigilance and insight leads them to notice traits of their partner which makes them realize that their partner's values simply do not match theirs and could cause major problems in the future.

A young born-again woman who starts to court a man, and finds out that he doesn't see the need for them to inform her Pastor of their relationship or intentions, and generally doesn't see the importance of her faith, should be commended when she decides to end that courtship.

It is rather a courting partner, who fails to spot or even hides obvious signs of major weaknesses in a relationship in order to get married, who may end up being a 'failure'.

BREAKING A RELATIONSHIP IS A BAD OMEN FOR YOUR FUTURE RELATIONSHIP

This is simply a myth and should be treated as such. Quitting a courtship does not in itself, have any direct bearing on your future marriage.

When done for the right reasons, quitting a courtship can rather demonstrate the person's ability to tackle major issues and make tough decisions.

PEOPLE WHO QUIT COURTSHIPS LACK PATIENCE AND UNDERSTANDING

Admittedly, there are those who walk out of courtships for flimsy reasons or reasons that can be resolved during the relationship. However, one cannot make the blanket statement as stated in this particular myth.

We live in a society where people have been encouraged to accept all sorts of unacceptable treatment including physical and sexual abuse in the name of 'patience and understanding'. These virtues – patience and understanding – are key to any lasting relationship; however, they are not to be used as a license for compromises that are ungodly, and sometimes rather damaging to the people involved in these relationships.

One has to understand that until one makes the final marriage vow, each of the partners have the right to decide against going on with the courtship without the whole world descending on them.

BREAKING A COURTSHIP IS PRACTISING DIVORCE

Yes, you may be wondering where that one came from! I sat back in shock one afternoon when someone came up with that one, whilst seeking counsel of how they were going to deal with a dilemma. This young woman had arrived at the conclusion that her relationship with a young man was wholly inappropriate and she wanted to walk away from it all. Her only problem was – she didn't want to practice divorce!

Thankfully, she found liberty in the truth that there was nothing like practicing divorce when it came to breaking courtships.

You are better off having a broken engagement than a broken marriage. It is important that we do not begin to equate courtship to a marriage – there has not been any exchange of vows.

It must also be said that if you are breaking up relationships just because you are 'testing the waters', then that behaviour is unacceptable.

SUSTAINING A COURTSHIP, EVEN IF UNHEALTHY, IS A SIGN OF LOVE AND COMMITMENT

How often have you seen someone keep an unhealthy courtship going at all costs – hiding information, sometimes even lying to their Pastors and friends in order to look good only for everything to crumble before their very eyes not long after marriage? At times like these, some Christians have quickly blamed the Devil for decisions even he did not influence!

Sometimes the decision to sustain an unhealthy courtship itself is a major sign of weakness which may haunt the person for the rest of their marriage. Love is wonderful, but tough love is wonderful at making tough decisions. There are times when the best manifestation of love in a courtship is to let individuals go their separate ways rather than 'kill' each other in a relationship.

When it comes to the issue of commitment, Christians ought to remember that our commitment to God should take priority over our commitment to any other person. Some have compromised God's word in the name of being committed to someone they have met, and have thereby ended up with disastrous results.

ONCE YOU ACCEPT A PROPOSAL YOU CANNOT GO BACK ON YOUR WORD, NO MATTER WHAT HAPPENS

It is funny how people are prepared to keep a courtship going at all costs in the name of keeping their word, and then suddenly lose the zeal to keep their word when they get married and start running into problems.

Prior to exchanging vows to seal the covenant of marriage, the partners are not under any obligation to remain in courtship under any circumstances. Simply put, since you are not yet married, you should not be acting as if you are in wedlock.

Other synonyms of the word 'proposal' are 'offer', 'suggestion', 'tender' and 'application'. All the above can be given, accepted, refused or withdrawn.

That is exactly what a marriage proposal is – 'offer', 'suggestion', 'tender' or 'application'. Do not let pressure from friends and family cause you to hold on to a courtship that you know is unhealthy, and which you need to withdraw from.

There are relationships that build you up, those that pull you down and those that drain your energy. The kind that drains you is what we refer to here as an unhealthy relationship.

We have been making references to relationships being unhealthy and will like us to have a look at some types of unhealthy relationships.

4 TYPES OF UNHEALTHY RELATIONSHIPS

FUNCTIONAL RELATIONSHIP

This is where a relationship has developed through to the courtship stage, but one partner's choice has been solely based on:

ca What their partner does

ca What their partner can do for them

ca What their partner has done in the past, and sadly not on who their partner actually is i.e. their personality.

The major problem with functional relationships is that the person who uses this criteria in making their decision forgets that the career of their partner can, and may change. People have been known to make career changes at certain stages of their lives and in some cases the changes are forced on them by external circumstances.

How does this kind of relationship survive if a partner's sole reason for being committed is that he or she wanted to marry a medical doctor or lawyer and somewhere along the line, the partner ends up becoming a full time Minister of the gospel?

If your decision seems to be solely based on what the other person is capable of doing for you – maybe catering for your financial needs right from the beginning, what would you do if this person hits a bad patch in their life and he or she is no longer capable of doing so?

In extreme cases, you hear of people in functional relationships who threaten their partner that they will walk away from the relationship if an immediate need is not catered for whilst they are in courtship! That is simply blackmail and very unhealthy.

PROMISCUOUS RELATIONSHIP

This is a kind of relationship where we end up sharing our bodies inappropriately. By this we mean, a courtship which results in regular sexual activity. As Christians, the word of God is our standard, and sex before marriage is frowned upon by the scriptures. Paul simply admonishes us and says quite simply, if you want to have sex get your own spouse and then you are free to have sex with him or her.

> *1 Corinthians 7:1-2 (NKJV) - Now concerning the things of which you wrote to me: It is good for a man not to touch a woman. Nevertheless, because of sexual immorality, let each man have his own wife, and let each woman have her own husband.*

Sometimes relationships have taken on a promiscuous nature because of a rather popular perception that the only way to keep a relationship going is through sexual activity. There are even a significant number of Christian men and women who have bought into this lie, that the way to keep a man or woman interested in a relationship is to offer him or her sex! Needless to say, some unscrupulous men have jumped at every opportunity to sell this theory to any woman who is ready to buy into it, just so as to have their way with them.

Women who have bought into this idea sometimes forget that even in marriage, it is possible that you could go through a period where you may not be available sexually to your partner. What then happens? Going by the same crooked theory, he should then be justified in sleeping with the next person he finds, shouldn't he? What will keep a man or woman interested in a relationship isn't simply sex, it is their fear of God.

CONTRACTUAL RELATIONSHIP

This is where courtship is used as a bargaining chip! This is the kind of relationship where we agree to an exchange of goods and services in a conditional contract. For example, you pay my fees through school and I am all yours!

> Do the right thing because it never pays to compromise – it costs and most of the time will cost you more than you can pay when it catches up with you.

I once came across the unfortunate story of Theresa (not her real name) who got married relatively early in life – at the age of 21 – and had major problems in the marriage. Upon further investigation, I discovered that whilst in school a young man gladly paid her fees and was regularly buying gifts for her mother.

He endeared himself to her mother for obvious reasons and as soon as Theresa finished school, she was 'encouraged' by her mother to marry this lawyer and church elder.

Little did the mother and Theresa know that this was the beginning of her torture. Physical and psychological abuse was the order of the day till they finally divorced two years later when she was 23 years old — completely traumatized. She once remarked, "his favourite time was very early in the morning. He would often beat me up without me even knowing the reason for it."

Learn to trust God for the right time. Trust God for the right person even if things are not working the way you want, and do what you need to do without compromising your faith. If you need to get another job to improve your financial situation, do so.

ADDICTIVE RELATIONSHIP

Relationships and especially those that develop into courtship are meant to be fun, as we mentioned earlier. However, this is not the case when you find yourself in an addictive relationship.

This is where a partner demands that the other partner meets his or her neurotic need. In other words, make me feel good about myself or else it is your fault. In such relationships, the people involved can become so absorbed in each other that they start to lose all their contacts with the outside world and start to suffocate each other.

Such relationships eventually drain the people involved of all their energy. It leaves them exhausted, miserable and unfulfilled. When courtships are run in this manner and they evolve into marriages, they tend to be miserable marriages.

Partners in such relationships depend almost solely on each other for everything and some mistake this for love and a deep sense of commitment to each other. It is unhealthy because you simply wear each other out eventually.

You cannot ask a man or woman to meet all the needs in your life. They simply cannot because no one has that capacity – only God does.

12 GUIDELINES FOR STEPPING UP FROM A BROKEN RELATIONSHIP

1. If you have to step out of a relationship, do it in a polite and graceful manner. The pain and uneasiness associated with ending a relationship is enough for you to add ridicule to it as well. Be assertive but polite.

2. Do not go announcing to friends and anyone who cares to listen, the weaknesses of your previous partner. Don't get caught up in a competition, with each partner trying to prove to the rest of the whole that they were the 'better' partner in the relationship. This is not a sign of maturity and must be avoided because it leaves people hurt and broken.

3. Understand that being part of a broken relationship does not make you a failure.

4. Seek assistance, if necessary, to seriously analyse the reasons for the breakup.

5. Do not rush into the 'ok, let's remain as friends' thing.

6. Do not replace the pain of the break-up with another relationship.

7. Do not go for a security blanket of other single friends who have become anti-relationships.

8. If sexual sin was prevalent in the relationship, seek forgiveness and restoration from God.

9. If the relationship was broken by an act of betrayal, seek help in dealing with the feeling of rejection.

10. If the relationship was abusive – verbally, sexually or physically – it is time to rebuild your self-esteem again.

11. If the break up was of a bitter nature, seek help in dealing with the psychological damage which the verbal abuse and other acts may have caused.

12. Learn to forgive and trust again. Trust is a necessary risk we all take if we are to build successful relationships. Although you have decided not to continue the relationship with this person, it pays to release that person in forgiveness as any bitterness you harbour threatens to poison your next relationship.

#6 – STUDY GUIDE

"People who have experienced broken courtships are failures". Discuss.

_____

_____

_____

_____

What are the signs of unhealthy relationships and which two are common, in your opinion?

_____

_____

_____

_____

What are the appropriate steps one should take in order to step out from a broken courtship?

_____

_____

_____

_____

Think Before You Wink

#7
SENSE AND NONSENSE OF SEX

The subject of sex and certainly open discussion about it is almost a taboo in most societies, let alone the church.

Dealing with this subject in the pulpit generates all sorts of reactions from people and most people feel very uneasy about having to hear it discussed in the church of all places. "Surely the church is the place reserved for holy conversations so why are we talking about sex," you can almost hear some exclaim.

This general attitude has left us in a situation where sex has become a silent topic in the pulpit but a rather loud activity in the pews! Ask any 21st century Pastor or Christian counsellor and they will agree that the significant number of cases they deal with has something to do with sex, in one way or the other.

Sex has therefore become the elephant in the room among Christians — too big that it is impossible to overlook, thus people just pretend it is not there because they have chosen to avoid dealing with it.

We often conduct a straw poll whenever we talk on this subject at events and we ask the question: 'Where did you get most of your knowledge about sex from — your parents, your local church, your friends or the media?"

Without exception, wherever I've been, not more than ten hands in a crowd of a thousand will be raised to say they learnt from parents and church, but when it comes to the options of friends and media, the air is filled with raised hands and mischievous smiles to go along with it.

We can therefore conclude that it appears what has shaped our views, even as Christians, hasn't been the church's teaching on sex, but friends (both good and bad ones, I may add) and the ever noisy media.

No wonder, most Pastors and Christian leaders battle with perceptions and ideas about sex which they find almost foreign to Christian values and principles. Simply put, since the church didn't teach them, someone else has taken the opportunity to teach them their own views on sex, and now the church is having to deal with the results of it.

We carry this mindset, which we may have picked up from friends or the media, into our adult relationships, including courtship as Christians, and we cling on to a number of myths that the world system has sold to us.

These myths have largely affected the way most people run their relationships, including courtships and we intend to take a close look at them in this chapter because we simply cannot continue to ignore them.

13 POPULAR MYTHS ABOUT SEX

This is in no way an exhaustive list of myths about sex, but a look at these key myths will go a long way to help us realign our perception of sex with biblical values.

GOD IS AGAINST SEX BECAUSE IT IS UNHOLY

This myth may be enforced by the apparent unwillingness of the church to talk about sex but God has never had a problem with sex. In fact, the first man and woman did not produce their children by 'fission' like the amoeba — a process where they simply divide in half producing two smaller daughter cells.

The King James Version uses the word 'knew'. Adam knew his wife, meaning he had intimate relations — sexual relations with her and she conceived and bore a son.

> *Genesis 4:1 (NKJV)* - *Now Adam knew Eve his wife, and she conceived and bore Cain, and said, "I have acquired a man from the Lord."*

We have made a fundamental mistake by associating sex with sin, because God created sex, and a study of the word of God clearly reveals He blessed sex in the context of marriage and frowns upon it outside of marriage. Sex is holy. It was created by the Holy One Himself.

SEX IS THE BEST WAY TO SHOW LOVE – EVEN IF YOU ARE NOT MARRIED

This myth has been used time and time again to convince unwilling partners to succumb to pre-marital sex, with statements like 'if you truly love me, you will have sex with me;' and 'it just shows how much I love you'.

Well, Jesus commented on the subject of showing love for one another.

> *John 15:13 (NKJV)* - *Greater love has no one than this, than to lay down one's life for his friends.*

If you love someone, you show it by being prepared to sacrifice for that person. You do not show it by getting them involved in something that will strain their relationship with God by causing them to sin.

Paul, writing to the Corinthians, stated clearly that marriage is the place for sexual activity. In the eyes of God, one is not entitled to sex just because he or she feels like it.

> *1 Corinthians 7:8-9 (NKJV)* - *But I say to the unmarried and to the widows: It is good for them if they remain even as I am; but if they cannot exercise self-control, let them marry. For it is better to marry than to burn with passion.*

Note here that Paul does not argue that 'if they cannot exercise self-control, let them have sex'. He says, 'let them marry'.

PRE-MARITAL SEX IS ALRIGHT AS LONG AS YOU INTEND TO MARRY

Once again this popular myth, a slight variation of the one previously mentioned, is normally used to soothe the conscience of most Christians when faced with the decision to engage in pre-marital sex. "After all, we will be getting married soon so God understands", they say.

Intending to marry, which is what gets one into courtship, is not marrying. Marrying is making the ultimate commitment before God and man. As we previously mentioned, intentions can be changed. So the person who convinces you to engage in pre-marital sex because you intend to marry can also turn round later and let you know that they have changed their minds when it is convenient for them. This has left many people feeling cheated because they have spent intimate moments with someone based on an 'intention' and not the 'commitment' that marriage demands.

PORNOGRAPHY PREPARES YOU FOR SEX IN MARRIAGE

The pornography industry has been growing in leaps and bounds over the decades and people have sought various ways to justify it. One myth that the Devil is busy selling to young Christians is that it is just part of the preparation towards marriage. After all, this is what one will be doing in marriage so one should start learning by watching how it is done. It almost sounds logical!

The scripture however clearly states that you and I have no business coveting someone or something that is not ours. Lusting after someone's daughter or son in pornography is a sin – contrary to God's word and we cannot justify it as preparation.

Matthew 5:28 (NKJV) - *But I say to you that whoever looks at a woman to lust for her has already committed adultery with her in his heart.*

The purpose of pornography is to arouse the viewer and you cannot be aroused without lusting after (wanting to have sex with) the person or persons you are watching in pornography.

PORNOGRAPHY IS JUST HARMLESS FUN

There used to be a time when those who wanted to view any form of pornography had to go great lengths to get it. In some countries, news agents and other shops were not allowed to display pornographic material on their shelves except at the very top shelves where you will have to purposefully go looking for them there to see it.

However, we are now in an era where it is very easily accessible on the internet and our so-called mainstream media, especially TV, is now happily dishing out a dose of it on a regular basis. Our dramas and movies are now no longer complete without some sex scenes.

The challenge for the Christian is this: One cannot hide from the fact that pornography arouses the viewer and increases his or her desire to engage in sex, so what are we doing regularly by watching and enjoying these and thinking that we will not be seeking for opportunities to practice it?

Romans 8:5-8 (NKJV) - *For those who live according to the flesh set their minds on the things of the flesh, but those who live according to the Spirit, the things of the Spirit. For to be carnally minded is death, but to be spiritually minded is life and peace. Because the carnal mind is enmity against God; for it is not subject to the law of God, nor indeed can be. So then, those who are in the flesh cannot please God.*

Pornography feeds the flesh and anything you feed, grows.

ONE NEEDS TO TEST FOR SEXUAL COMPATIBILITY BEFORE MARRIAGE

This myth has been gaining grounds rapidly because of the image the world seems to project to us, that sex is the most important thing in marriage and in fact it is what really matters about relationships in this life.

We now live in a world that is going crazy about sex. There is the impression that everyone is doing it and so you need to be outdoing the person next to you. We call it 'having fun'.

Those who fall for this myth fail to realise that, apart from it being a sin before God which we have established with earlier myths, one has to value oneself to the point of understanding that you are not for 'testing'.

Once again, the whole concept of testing means there are three possible outcomes – success, failure, inconclusive results which may require further testing! After this so-called testing, both the 'tester' and 'tested' can walk away into other relationships because there hasn't been any marriage, just an intent.

What most young women do not grasp is that the same gentleman who is insisting on testing for sexual compatibility will not be prepared to marry someone who has been 'tested' by several people!

Remember, even cars become devalued when used for test driving, how much more a human being, fearfully and wonderfully created by God?

A MAN WILL LOVE A WOMAN MORE IF HE MAKES LOVE TO HER

The term 'making love' makes sex sound so wonderful, but sex and love are two completely different things.

If this myth was to be true, then prostitutes will be the most loved on our planet. But why is it that most of them are broken and end up hating themselves, and in some cases have to ply themselves with alcohol and drugs just to keep them going?

Does the rapist fall in love with his victim because he has raped her? Sex, on its own, does not bind people together.

> *2 Samuel 13:14-16 (NKJV) - However, he would not heed her voice; and being stronger than she, he forced her and lay with her. Then Amnon hated her exceedingly, so that the hatred with which he hated her was greater than the love with which he had loved her. And Amnon said to her, "Arise, be gone!" So she said to him, "No, indeed! This evil of sending me away is worse than the other that you did to me." But he would not listen to her.*

After Amnon had raped Tamar, he rather hated her and threw her out of his house! How many times have Christian women secretly suffered such humiliation because they fell for this myth that "he will love me more if I sleep with him?"

YOU CANNOT KEEP A MAN OR WOMAN IN COURTSHIP WITHOUT HAVING SEX WITH HIM OR HER

This is another popular myth which has led most people to believe that the most effective way to keep a person in a relationship with you is to have sex with them regularly.

Firstly, one needs to understand as stated earlier that pre-marital sex is a sin before God, and that fact cannot change.

Secondly, those who become believers in this myth also fail to realize that a person who subscribes to this school of thought can also easily have sex with someone else once they feel they are bored with you.

For people like this, their desire for sexual gratification exceeds their commitment to their relationship with you and with God so they are ready to do anything to fulfil their sexual desire.

MEN CANNOT CONTROL THEIR SEXUAL URGE ONCE THEY FIND SOMEONE ATTRACTIVE

This is another myth that some men have used to justify why they should engage in pre-marital sex with their fiancée. Some have even used this to eventually force themselves on their fiancées!

We've come across women who, in a perverse sort of way, have believed this myth to the extent that they use it to justify their fiancé's inappropriate behaviour towards them. "Oh, when he sees me he cannot control himself. He says I am irresistible", they say, wearing silly smiles.

If a man cannot control himself when he finds someone attractive, there is a surprise for you. When he gets married, he will be having the same problem. One shocking fact most men will not admit publicly (for good reasons too) is that after marrying someone, you are bound to find someone else in this world of 7 billion people who is possibly more attractive than your wife!

So not even marriage can protect someone with this mentality. Some have argued that once they are married they will not encounter any such challenges because their wives will be available. Well, there are times she simply wouldn't be. The scripture admonishes us to control our sexual urge.

> *Colossians 3:5-6 (NKJV)* - *Therefore put to death your members which are on the earth: fornication, uncleanness, passion, evil desire, and covetousness, which is idolatry. Because of these things the wrath of God is coming upon the sons of disobedience.*

MEN CANNOT FUNCTION PROPERLY IN LIFE WITHOUT SEXUAL ACTIVITY

Firstly, there have been no research findings or a case of a man dying for lack of sex contrary to what this myth will have us believe.

Paul, in his writing to the Corinthians, encouraged those who could, to emulate him by not being married, because it was possible. It could be done.

> *1 Corinthians 7:7-8 (NKJV)* - *For I wish that all men were even as I myself. But each one has his own gift from God, one in this manner and another in that. But I say to the unmarried and to the widows: It is good for them if they remain even as I am.*

Contrary to what the media and the rest of the world may be portraying, not everyone is doing it. Do not be deceived into believing this myth.

HEAVY PETTING IS ALRIGHT AS LONG AS IT DOES NOT RESULT IN SEX

This is where two people have very intimate sexual contact with each other but avoid penetrative sex.

This myth bases its argument on the fact that as long as there hasn't been penetrative sex, all is well. However, yielding to this puts the couple in a position where they become aroused and by so doing their inhibition is greatly reduced.

Once their inhibition starts to give way, their judgment is clouded and they can easily cross the boundary to penetrative sex.

Also, the scripture makes mention of 'uncleanness' in addition to fornication, and such behaviour can be classified as such because it leads us into activity that keeps us so close to fornication that our consciences are pricked.

> *Ephesians 5:2-3 (NKJV) - And walk in love, as Christ also has loved us and given Himself for us, an offering and a sacrifice to God for a sweet-smelling aroma. But fornication and all uncleanness or covetousness, let it not even be named among you, as is fitting for saints;*

ORAL SEX IS NOT SEX SO IT IS ALRIGHT OUTSIDE MARRIAGE

It is becoming increasingly common to come across young men and women who believe in this myth. Once again, the subject of uncleanness comes up here.

At a recent seminar we taught in, I was asked this question and the questioner appeared to be of this persuasion and was arguing that there really was nothing wrong with it because it wasn't a sin.

I decided to reflect it back to the questioner by suggesting that, if it was truly harmless then I will not expect him to be the least bothered if he married his fiancée and one day chanced upon his wife doing same with her boss, since 'there is nothing wrong with it'! He didn't find it very funny but later got the point.

Oral sex is sexual, and we should not be using each other in such a manner outside marriage.

> *1 Thessalonians 4:3-7 (NKJV)* - *For this is the will of God, your sanctification: that you should abstain from sexual immorality; that each of you should know how to possess his own vessel in sanctification and honor, not in passion of lust, like the Gentiles who do not know God; that no one should take advantage of and defraud his brother in this matter, because the Lord is the avenger of all such, as we also forewarned you and testified. For God did not call us to uncleanness, but in holiness.*

IT IS ALRIGHT TO MASTURBATE WHILST WAITING TO GET MARRIED

This has become another hotly debated subject in our society today. Masturbation is simply stimulating one's sexual organ till the person reaches the point of orgasm.

Just like oral sex, the bible does not specifically mention masturbation as a sin but one of the main issues for us to consider as Christian men and women is what goes into the act itself.

Firstly, the imagery the person tends to focus on whilst masturbating. The individual tends to fantasize or lust after someone as they go through this act and that in itself is not pleasing to God.

> *Matthew 5:28 (NKJV)* - *But I say to you that whoever looks at a woman to lust for her has already committed adultery with her in his heart.*

This tendency to focus on images leads most people who masturbate to also use pornography.

Secondly, this is a habit that can become addictive so quickly that it starts to fill one's mind with sexual images and feed the flesh. The person's spiritual life starts to suffer as a result.

GOD CREATED EACH OF US TO BE SEXUAL

As mentioned previously, sex was created by God and so it should come as no surprise to us when we discover that we have sexual feelings. It is not demonic or devilish in any way – it is how God made us.

Sex is what God created as our means of reproduction.

> *Genesis 4:1 (NKJV)* - *Now Adam knew Eve his wife, and she conceived and bore Cain, and said, "I have acquired a man from the Lord."*

5 TRUTHS ABOUT GOD'S VIEW ON SEX EVERY CHRISTIAN SINGLE SHOULD KNOW

SEX WITHIN MARRIAGE IS GREAT

Someone once joked that apart from the experience of salvation, sex is the next best thing God created for us! Sex is not to be seen as dirty if it is enjoyed within the covenant of marriage. In fact, the scripture encourages married couples to have sex.

> *Proverbs 5:18-21 (NKJV)* - *Let your fountain be blessed, and rejoice with the wife of your youth. As a loving deer and a graceful doe, Let her breasts satisfy you at all times; And always be enraptured with her love. For why should you, my son, be enraptured by an immoral woman, and be embraced in the arms of a seductress? For the ways of man are before the eyes of the Lord, and He ponders all his paths.*

SEX IS A CELEBRATION OF THE MARRIAGE COVENANT

As partners of the marriage covenant, the husband and wife owe it to each other to be sexually available to each other as a celebration of the covenant.

Sex is therefore an integral part of every marriage.

> *1 Corinthians 7:3-4 (NKJV)* - *Let the husband render to his wife the affection due her, and likewise also the wife to her husband. The wife does not have authority over her own body, but the husband does. And likewise the husband does not have authority over his own body, but the wife does.*

SEX RESULTS IN THE BONDING OF THE BODY, SOUL AND SPIRIT

Contrary to popular belief, sexual intercourse is not just a physical thing. It goes well beyond that.

> *1 Corinthians 6:15-16 (NKJV)* - *Do you not know that your bodies are members of Christ? Shall I then take the members of Christ and make them members of a harlot? Certainly not! Or do you not know that he who is joined to a harlot is one body with her? For "the two," He says, "shall become one flesh."*

SEX DOES NOT MAKE A MARRIAGE. IT IS THE QUALITY OF INTIMACY IN A MARRIAGE THAT MAKES MARITAL SEX WONDERFUL.

Great friendship results in great intimacy which in turn makes sex wonderful. Instead of focusing on so-called 'sexual compatibility', if we were to focus on building great friendships during courtship, we would be setting ourselves up for great sex in marriage.

> *Song of Songs 5:16 (NKJV)* - *His mouth is most sweet, Yes, he is altogether lovely. This is my beloved, and this is my friend, O daughters of Jerusalem!*

Which five of the popular myths about sex have you personally heard and how do you think it has influenced your perception of sexual relations?

_____

_____

_____

_____

Does God really consider sex as holy and acceptable? If so, why is it that most of us are uncomfortable discussing sex?

_____

_____

_____

_____

Is premarital sex acceptable as long as the partners involved intend to marry each other? Discuss

_____

_____

_____

_____

#8 QUESTIONS AND ANSWERS

Over the years, we have met many singles in various events, and the question and answer sessions have always been the highlight. We will like to share just a few with you. Do not be judgmental of the people who ask certain questions. The quality of the questions a person asks gives an indication of their level or the light available to them. It also gives one an indication of the challenges they may be going through.

It is our prayer that the answers to some of these questions will be a blessing to you.

QUESTION 1

What happens when the lady you have in mind is of a different religion?

Being of a different religion is very significant and as a born-again Christian you need to enter the marriage covenant with a person who shares your faith (See 2 Corinthians 6:14,15 and Amos 3:3)

QUESTION 2

Is sex vital in courtship?

As born-again Christians, we are not supposed to have sex during courtship. Sex before marriage is termed as fornication which scripture clearly describes at sin. Do not let anyone deceive you with theories about 'testing sexual compatibility!'

QUESTION 3

Do you need to be friends before proposing?

We strongly advise that you develop friendship with a person before proposing because it is unwise to invite someone into a lifetime covenant such as marriage without even knowing them.

QUESTION 4

Is 10 years a significant age difference between me and my prospective wife who I know loves and honours God beyond all reasonable doubt?

Ten years gap is not a definite reason not to marry an individual. However, there are key issues you should address. Are you ready to understand her world — for example relate to her friends (who may be 10years or more younger than you)? Will you be able to respect her and treat her as a wife instead of a younger sister or even a daughter?

QUESTION 5

What do you do if you find out that someone you broke up with has suddenly become nice to you again four months later?

Firstly, what was the reason for the break-up? Secondly, what exactly do you mean by 'being nice to you'? If it is about the person trying to restore the relationship, then you should make your decision based on your review of your reasons for the initial break-up.

QUESTION 6

Is it advisable to marry someone that I met on the internet who I have not seen physically but communicates with on the phone? He is born-again and we are from the same country although based abroad.

We will strongly advise you not to commit to marriage proposals from someone you've never met in person since a personality on the internet and phone can be anyone (even if they send you photographs). Firstly, you cannot guarantee their identity and secondly, you will need to meet them and have a better idea of their own environment before committing to them in marriage.

QUESTION 7

Do you have to marry someone whose native language you do not understand? I ask this because how will the person react if family members come around and start speaking this language that they don't understand?

Firstly, there should be no problem as long as the two individuals have a common language which they can communicate in (it could even be English). The onus also lies on the person whose family is speaking this language to make his spouse feel a part of what is going on, despite the language barrier.

QUESTION 8

Could you please make us understand that courtship should not be treated as marriage because most of my lady friends don't seem to agree? They argue that it must be treated as marriage sometimes to keep the man.

Firstly, what exactly do you mean by 'treated as marriage'? If it means having sex with him, you are first sinning against God, and secondly, you run the risk of cheapening yourself. Sex doesn't bind a man to marry you – he could just walk away. If it means being possessive, it can actually backfire since it makes the courtship rather tiresome and unattractive.

QUESTION 9

Sometimes it is very difficult to know everything, especially the bad habits of your partner during courtship, which could eventually crop up in marriage. Is it possible to know all about your partner in courtship?

No, it is not possible to know all about your partner in courtship. However, there are always key signals which one should look out for as we discussed during the Summit. For example, evidence of ungodly values such as dishonesty, unfaithfulness and violence should warn you of imminent danger.

QUESTION 10

I have hardly been friends with guys. I have just had a few and I realize that I fantasize about all of them even though I don't want to be in a romantic relationship with them. Am I sinning?

Assuming that these fantasies are of a sexual nature, Matt 5:28 admonishes us not to dwell on such fantasies as they are sin in themselves (by the way, it works both ways – men or women). You will need to seek counselling to deal with this specific issue of fantasizing as you need to bring your mind under subjection to God's word. (2 Corinthians 10:5)

QUESTION 11

How do you deal with a broken heart? (My fiancée broke up with me and even though it happened a year ago, I am still in pain and it is affecting my current relationship)

It is always advisable not to enter into another relationship whilst healing from the first break up. It is important to deal with the hurt, anger and resentment that resulted from the break up. It is also a time to examine yourself and see if there is anything you need to work on, obviously depending on the reason for the break up in the first place. It is advisable to see a counsellor to walk you through a process of healing and forgiveness.

QUESTION 12

I have a boyfriend who is married, but promised to divorce his wife and marry me. He says he doesn't love his wife. Should I continue with our relationship? I am confused because, he has been of great support to me and I am scared that if I break up with him, he might stop helping me one way or the other.

Well, first things first, he is married already. He's someone's husband and you are assisting him in the breakdown of that union. You should not date a married man, period! What God has joined together let no man separate. Always remember, never let any man use what he has to buy your love and loyalty, because it is the wrong foundation to build any relationship on. You must wait for the right man who is not married to come along. Also remember, there is no guarantee that he will leave his wife and get married to you. Don't build your life on false hopes. Leave this man and let him sort out the problems he has with his wife.

QUESTION 13

A male friend of mine proposed to me. And whilst waiting for my response, I found out that he was getting closer and befriending a close friend of mine. Please what do I do since I've noticed that my female friend's attitude towards me appears to have changed radically recently?

Firstly, you have not accepted his proposal so he doesn't have any indication that you are interested in being in a relationship with him. If you are, you better speak up. Secondly, the fact that he seems to be befriending your friend will obviously make you uncomfortable but until you let him know where you stand on the proposal, you will not know for sure if he has decided to move on or not.

QUESTION 14

I was sexually abused some years ago and since then, I have developed a phobia for sex. Is it advisable for me to let my fiancé know during courtship or do I wait till marriage?

Sexual abuse can have a traumatic effect on the victim. Firstly, you will need to see a professional counsellor to help you deal with the effects, and you should not wait till you are in courtship to do this. Secondly, this is something you should disclose to your counsellor or Pastor during pre-marital counselling so that the Pastor will help both of you through it. If your fiancé is not emotionally matured enough, just telling him may cause him to withdraw. The Pastor and/or the counsellor will be of help through this process.

QUESTION15

I recently read about a scientific discovery of certain sequences of genes which manifest themselves in a disposition to homosexuality. I nearly ruled that out until I learnt of a devout Christian worker who confessed to having such a disposition. If a person has such a disposition, can they live a sincere Christian life?

The debate about this supposed discovery is still raging between the various camps in the genetic research world and the existence of this sequence cannot be said to be conclusive in any way. Secondly, learning of a devout Christian confessing that he is disposed to homosexuality does not necessarily support this theory. To live a sincere Christian life is not to perform Christian rituals but to obey the word of God. There is ample evidence in the word of God that shows that although God loves everyone, He calls homosexuality a sin. There are also cases of people who have confessed to be ex-homosexuals who are now born-again and are living in heterosexual relationships.

QUESTION 16

Please, at what age can I start courting? I am 24 years old and in my third year in school.

Firstly, this is dependent to some extent on the cultural setting in which you've grown up. Some people in the Western world have been known to start relationships that lead to courtships from as early as 18yrs old. Those in certain parts of Africa may wait longer; others even become child brides (something we do not recommend). However, the important factor to consider is whether you are ready to make the emotional investment that such relationships demand from you. If you are, then 24years is not too early to start courting.

QUESTION 17

Is it right to accept a marriage proposal on a first date?

No. This is simply because you need to take time to know more about this individual before you accept a marriage proposal from them.

QUESTION 18

After listening to all that you have to say at this seminar, I have come to a conclusion that I am in the wrong kind of relationship. Am I too late in breaking this relationship since I have already had sex with this person?

Knowingly continuing in this unhealthy relationship will rather make things worse for you. The fact that you have had sex with this person does not mean that you are stuck with them forever. You sinned with them and you need to go to God for forgiveness and restoration but as long as you have not married them yet, you are free to break it off.

QUESTION 19

Can one end a courtship that both extended families are aware of?

Yes. The extended families being aware of a courtship may make it a bit more difficult to break but never impossible. Remember, you are not choosing the person for your extended family. You are making a decision you will be living with for the rest of your life, so that should be the priority. If you are convinced that the courtship cannot be improved even through counselling then it is time to act. Your extended families will eventually get used to the decision.

QUESTION 20

I want to know if it is ok for me to assist my man in washing and other household duties when he is seriously sick and there are no immediate relatives or friends to assist him?

Well, in exceptional cases like this, one can assist. However, it should be the exception and not the norm. This should not be the excuse to get you acting like a wife in the gentleman's home. Ask yourself the question, if he were not in a relationship with you, what would he have done?

QUESTION 21

What if your prospective spouse is a genuine Christian but your prospective in-laws are of a different faith? Should one go ahead in courtship in this case?

Yes, it is ok to go ahead with this person. You are marrying the person not their parents and as long as this person is not the kind that is overly influenced by their parents, you shouldn't have any issues with this.

QUESTION 22

My sister's ex-boyfriend is asking me out. Is it advisable to go out with him since he is no longer with my sister?

Technically speaking, if he is no longer dating your sister then he is free to go out with anyone of his choice– including you. However, there are various issues you should be taking into consideration. Why did his relationship with your sister break up? If the break up was a bitter one, how do you intend reconciling your relationship with this gentleman and your relationship with your sister. If you were to marry this man, how will it play out within your family? You may find out after looking at these issues that it is simply not worth the complications.

QUESTION 23

Is it right to date a man or woman who is not as spiritually matured as you are?

As Christians, we believe that the word of God gives the husband the role of being the head of the home. This is not an excuse for one to lord it over their wives or abuse them, but to offer leadership, including spiritual leadership. So for a man who has to marry a woman who is not as spiritually matured, it is not really a problem because he can lead and nurture his wife spiritually. Where it is the man who is not as spiritually matured, the woman has to be sure that the man is genuinely keen on growing spiritually, or else she will run into problems in marriage.

QUESTION 24

My fiancée left me for someone else at a time when I felt I needed her most in my life. Should we still be friends?

This is a difficult experience to deal with. Firstly, you have to learn to forgive her, as difficult as it may sound. Secondly, you are not under any obligation to be friends with this person and so you should focus on healing the hurt you are experiencing first. You can always re-define your friendship with this person later and it doesn't have to be a close friendship if her presence in your life is going to be a constant reminder of the betrayal.

QUESTION 25

How healthy is a courtship of 6years without meeting the parents of my fiancé? He keeps saying he is not ready and he is the shy type.

Six years is far too long to be hanging around in courtship! And being shy and not ready is a rather weak excuse for him not introducing you to his parents after six years. This situation is unhealthy and he needs to take immediate steps to rectify the situation because there is also the danger that he may be hiding something from you.

QUESTION 26

As a born-again, spirit-filled Christian lady, I have had a lot of Christian men wanting to marry me but I want God's choice for my life. All the men who have approached me are God-fearing. Do I have to choose the best based on my own taste and preferences because they all seem to meet my criteria?

After you have prayed for God to give you guidance, the decision as to who to marry still rests with you. You can only marry one of them so the earlier you make a decision, the better. Make sure you evaluate your criteria to ensure you are focusing on the right things such as the non-negotiable and the negotiable (see Chapter 3). You are not going to marry a perfect person and having done this prayerfully, you cannot be waiting for a writing on the wall. Make a decision.

QUESTION 27

Please how do you cope with a guy who can't seem to be able to say no to ladies' requests? My boyfriend confessed to me that he can't just say no to ladies because he respects ladies. He sometimes gets involved in helping ex-girlfriends even to his own detriment.

I think both of you need to seek counsel because your boyfriend needs to have a balance in his life. Is he going to these extents because he likes to have the attention of these ladies and to be seen as the solution to everyone's problems? Has he considered your feelings in all these? Are you ready to deal with a husband who seems to jump at everyone else's request even to the detriment of his own marriage?

QUESTION 28

How do you break off a relationship with a married man?

You have no business being in that kind of a relationship with a married man. So tell him enough is enough and cut off your contact with him as much as possible. You need to give yourself a rude shock by cutting off completely so you can wean yourself off him or else you will end up in a rather messy situation.

QUESTION 29

I'm dating this guy, he takes care of my financial needs. Because of this he doesn't respect me. He talks to me anyhow and is always asking for space anytime I question him about his relationship with other ladies. He says, I am too jealous and insecure. I am confused but I love him. What should I do? He has now asked that we end the relationship, should I let him go?

There seems to be a lack of respect for you in this relationship and it does stem from the fact that your boyfriend has taken on responsibilities for your needs. It's no longer a relationship of equals. You need to end the relationship and let him go. It might mean that you will experience a period of hardship because the financial support will come to an end. But you are better off with your self-esteem being intact than trying to hold on to a relationship in which you are being disrespected. Get a job and start earning some money for yourself. You are a person of value. God has blessed you with gifts and abilities. Learn how to fend for yourself. It will be a great asset when you eventually get married.

QUESTION 30

If a woman in courtship is not supposed to carry out certain chores for the man she is courting, how do I know that the woman I am about to marry can perform common household chores?

Your time of courtship is not a period for your fiancée to carry out common household chores on your behalf. It is a time to study each other, pray together and learn to understand each other's differences. If you really want to know whether she can take on common household chores, study how she takes care of her current environment. Remember, no one is perfect. If we had to test every man and woman on their suitability to be a wife or husband, no one would qualify.

QUESTION 31

Do tribal differences matter in marriage?

No. It only becomes an issue if you make it one. We are all one in Christ and despite our cultural differences, two people can build a successful marriage if they learn to appreciate each other and their respective cultures whilst making God's word their standard.

QUESTION 32

How best do you enjoy your life as a single person?

It is amazing how most singles spend most of their time wishing they were married and dreaming of what they would do, whilst there are a number of married people also secretly wishing they were single again so they could do what they missed out on!

As a single person, you have a degree of freedom and independence most married people do not have — make use of it! Study what you want to study, travel where you want to visit, spend time with friends and enjoy life to its fullest. Commit yourself to service in your local church — Eccl 12:1

QUESTION 33

There is this guy at my work place who has been giving me attention but has not asked me out. I think I like him. Now, is it advisable for me to ask him out as a woman or make my intentions known to him?

Firstly, this guy has not asked you out or made any approach and so you should be careful you are not reading meanings into what may turn out to be innocent actions. Get to know him just as a friend and that will give you a better opportunity to know more about him, and also for him to make his intentions known one way or the other. In most cultures, men frown on women who ask men out and in a case where he hasn't said anything, it is premature to be considering the man.

QUESTION 34

I am in a relationship with a lady who subsequently travelled. It has been 3 months and I have not even received a single phone call. I am therefore considering walking out of this relationship. Please advise me.

Yes, three months without any communication is odd but you should also be careful that you don't jump to conclusions too quickly. You need to exhaust all the possible options such as contacting her close family and friends to check what is happening. You owe it to yourself to establish that she has decided on her own free will to stop communicating with you before you take such a step.

QUESTION 35

Six and a half years ago, we agreed to marry. So I helped her through her University course and then after, a year's training course. We then sent letters round to get her a job. Six months after getting a job, I was informed of her wedding to another man on that very wedding day! A month later, she came to me apologizing and asking for further financial help. I have learnt the mistakes I made from this Summit. Should I still be friends with such a person?

This is undoubtedly a terrible experience and I am glad you have learnt your mistakes. Firstly, I pray that others will learn from your experience. Secondly, you need the grace of God to help you forgive her and this is not something that happens overnight. Thirdly, you should not be in a rush to maintain a friendship with her — you are hurt and you need healing. Finally, note that you are not under any obligation to keep her as a friend or you may suffer more hurt, as she seems to be expecting financial help again. It will be a greater disaster if you keep hanging around her and find yourselves attracted to each other again! Move on with your life. ·

#9
FINAL
THOUGHTS

We trust that the few things which God has enabled us to share with you in this book will serve as a useful guide as you go through this phase of your lives. The current trends in our society has put much pressure on what we know as traditional Christian principles and values, and it is our prayer that God will give us the grace to encourage each other to take a bold stand for Him in a world where compromise seems to be the order of the day.

The family is the bedrock of our society and as such the Devil will do anything to fight this institution called marriage. Marriages have therefore faced major challenges all over the world but one of the key reasons for this is that most marriages have started on the wrong footing.

As long as Christians continue to use the world's standards and values to manage their relationships, the results we produce in our marriages will be no different from what pertains outside the church.

True transformation will only come when we realign our mindset with the word of God rather than current prevailing trends set by our society.

Romans 12:1-2 (NKJV) - *I beseech you therefore, brethren, by the mercies of God, that you present your bodies a living sacrifice, holy, acceptable to God, which is your reasonable service. And do not be conformed to this world, but be transformed by the renewing of your mind, that you may prove what is that good and acceptable and perfect will of God.*

May God strengthen all of us as we resolve to stand for Him. God bless you!

Andy and Helen Yawson can be contacted by email on thinkb4youwink@yahoo.com

www.ingramcontent.com/pod-product-compliance
Lightning Source LLC
Chambersburg PA
CBHW081632040426

42449CB00014B/3282